ather, Berna and Frank Kavanaugh
rts ❀ Rudi Baumfeld, my mentor ❀
❀ books and more books ❀ Japan
Turner, and Brian Watkins ❀ Paul
Sister Corita Kent ❀ Patty Good
wman family ❀ drawing ❀ any kind
r, and Aiko Cuneo ❀ Andean tex-
ejza ❀ Edward James's Las Pozas
❀ Eudorah Moore ❀ Overton Park
urt Square in M   Indian
ictoria Lautman   on the
, Ireland ❀ Mary, Molly, Fran, and
tsen and family ❀ chairs ❀ tables
❀ Joseph Cornell ❀ toys ❀ vernac-
exico ❀ Carl Benkert ❀ fairy tales
any alphabet ❀ Elise Crawford ❀
rea ❀ Cranbrook Academy of Art
Richard Halliburton, *The Royal*
dget Burke ❀ Giovanna Garzoni ❀
karsgard ❀ Eero Saarinen's office

public affairs!

a colorful life
gere kavanaugh, designer

louise sandhaus and kat catmur
original photography by jennifer cheung

princeton architectural press
new york

**CAPTIONS FOR
PRECEDING PAGES**

P1: An ink-on-paper
drawing, *Gere
Kavanaugh*, by her friend,
the artist Ruth Asawa,
ca. 1965. Kavanaugh
met Asawa early in
the artist's career and
commissioned work
from her for several
projects.

P2: The elusive smile of
Gere Kavanaugh,
mid-1960s.

P3 Top: Kavanaugh in
her studio in the late
1960s. Above her are
samples from her Koryo
silk collection for Isabel
Scott Fabrics and, on the
wall, concept drawings
for Sonotube furniture
and play structures.

P3 Bottom: Kavanaugh
in front of a mock-up of
supergraphics designed
by Deborah Sussman for
a Joseph Magnin store,
ca. 1968. Kavanaugh,
Sussman, and their
studio mate Frank
Gehry were hired for the
project.

P4: A contact sheet
of photographs taken
at the studio Kavanaugh
shared with Frank Gehry
and Deborah Sussman on
San Vicente Boulevard in
West Los Angeles in the
mid-1960s.

P6: In a photograph
taken by her mentor, Rudi
Baumfeld, around 1965,
Kavanaugh visits the San
Francisco outlet of the
groundbreaking retailer
Design Research.

P7: Kavanaugh makes
herself at home in an
Eames lounge chair in
1966.

P8: During a 1964 trip to
Honduras, Kavanaugh
wears a dress (and textile)
of her own design. As a
guest of the United States
Agency for International
Development, Kavanaugh
worked with local
craftspeople to produce
goods for the American
market, such as these
straw hats. She spent
two months in Honduras,
along with several other
design ambassadors.

P12: HAIL TO BEA LEA, MID-
1970s. One of a number
of designs created for
Kavanaugh's own textile
line, Geraldine Fabrics.

contents

A Life in Color!
Louise Sandhaus

Colorful! California design queen Gere Kavanaugh (or Geré, as she often identified herself throughout her career) is as vibrant as a rainbow, with a spectrum of passions, creating visions just as bright. Behind Kavanaugh's brilliance is a lifetime of curiosity—about virtually anything and everything. Known for her acute powers of observation, she is never short of an opinion, or at least a pointed question. She always has something insightful to say, and she says it with that certain *oomph* that belongs to all larger-than-life creative figures. Her irrepressible, kaleidoscopic vision channels the magic of the universe into an alchemical mixture of creativity and imagination. Our lives would be gloomy without the Gere Kavanaughs of the world to show us how to look— to see—through their special lenses. ❊ And yet, amazingly, this is the first monograph devoted to her life and work, which are so blended that it's difficult to tell where one ends and the other begins: Kavanaugh the person is Kavanaugh the designer.

To describe Kavanaugh is to evoke all that "colorful" can: vivid, lively, animated, dramatic, fascinating, interesting, stimulating, scintillating. Her arrival is always announced with a distinctive "halloooooooo" and a whooping laugh. No shrinking violet, she is perfectly represented by one of her favorite motifs—the bright and optimistic daisy. ❊ Tall and commanding, with California sunset- red hair that remained flame-colored into her later years, she has been a mighty presence in the Los Angeles design scene since 1960. And she has always dressed for the show, whether clad in her own designs or costumed in garb from different cultures. Over the years the boundary between Kavanaugh's collection and her closet has blurred, and something that begins on her wall—a patchwork

Seminole shirt, bags with intricately woven geometric patterns,
beaded and felted footwear—might make its way to her wardrobe. And,
oh yeah, there was also that rubber-chicken purse... ✿ Naturally,
"colorful" also describes her work. Color has been an essential ele-
ment of her projects and the constant subject of her research. Her
move to Los Angeles in 1960 only deepened her obsession with color,
as she absorbed and reflected the vibrant hues of her Southern
California environment. After that moment everything went bright.
✿ And yet, well before she was a designer, Kavanaugh had a passion
for color; as a girl she'd stack her mother's spools of thread to
find pleasing combinations. With her submission to The Box Project—
an initiative begun by the Lloyd Cotsen Collection in 2004 that
invited artists to create a work that would fit into a small box—
Kavanaugh paid tribute to her mother for inspiring the first stanza
of her long and poetic career.

Gere Kavanaugh's 2010 untitled
contribution to the Cotsen
Collection's Box Project.

Home Is Where the (Design) Heart Is

Kavanaugh knows EVERYONE, and everyone seems to know her. Her home is a trove of folk art and vintage objects, of hand-sewn dolls and papier-mâché creatures, baskets, funnels, and kitchen implements of every ilk. Around Christmas, Kavanaugh's penchant for visual festivity goes into double-overdrive with an abundance of crèches and ornaments. And then there's the Hero Wall, a tribute and testament to her warm and impressive connections around the world. Among the senders of letters and photos are architect and inventor Buckminster Fuller, Beat artist Wallace Berman, photographer Imogen Cunningham, former Sinn Féin President Gerry Adams, and many mention-worthy more. ❁ Kavanaugh cheers for friends and colleagues from the front row at design events, and she gathers them around herself at home, hosting lively conversations, homemade culinary celebrations, and epic feasts where visual delights abound.

A Many-Hued Career

Born in Memphis, Tennessee, in 1929, Kavanaugh recalls an idyllic upbringing. Her father turned a passion for books into a later-in-life career as a rare book dealer, and her mother, at one time a seamstress, was a font of support throughout her daughter's life. Both parents cultivated her intrinsic awareness and curiosity, enrolling her at the Memphis Academy of Arts at the age of eight. Kavanaugh would stay at the school until she completed her undergraduate studies in 1951. ❁ Though Kavanaugh was recommended for a scholarship to Parsons School of Design in New York by none other than the director of the Metropolitan Museum of Art, Francis Henry Taylor, she chose instead to attend graduate school at Cranbrook Academy of Art in Bloomfield Hills, Michigan, after reading about the school in *Arts & Architecture* magazine. Attracted by Cranbrook's freedom of study, she applied without her parents' knowledge, and in the fall of 1951, with a loan from the C. M. Gooch Foundation, Kavanaugh moved to the bucolic campus. Tight finances mandated that she fast-track her studies, and she graduated from the cross-disciplinary design program—only the third woman to do so—at summer's end in 1952. ❁ After graduating, Kavanaugh was immediately recruited by General Motors to join its Styling group, the famously inventive division led by Harley Earl. She became part of a group of women that would later be promoted by GM as the

"Damsels of Design." There she conceived graphics, model kitchens, and dazzling trade show displays. ✿ Around 1954 Kavanaugh took a break from GM to work in the Detroit offices of Victor Gruen, the so-called father of the shopping mall. Headquartered in Los Angeles, Gruen Associates had established the Detroit satellite office to handle the considerable mall developments in the area for which he'd been commissioned. Kavanaugh returned to GM about a year later and remained there until 1958, when she left to pursue her own fortunes. ✿ Both her first solo venture and her time in Michigan came to a close in 1960 when she became head of interiors at Gruen in Los Angeles. There, under the mentorship of architect and partner Rudi Baumfeld, she designed interiors for department stores, including Joseph Magnin, an exclusive retail chain. She continued to work with Joseph Magnin even after she left the firm in 1964 and launched Gere Kavanaugh/Designs in a space shared with her former Victor Gruen colleague, architect Frank Gehry, and his University of Southern California former classmate Greg Walsh. ✿ Once she had established her own practice, Kavanaugh blossomed. The Cranbrook ethos of fearlessly tackling any design problem, no matter the discipline, had helped to form an eager risk-taker who never wavered and who refused to be bound by limitations. Gere Kavanaugh/Designs continues to flourish to this day and has produced everything from retail and residential interiors to textiles, graphics, furniture, exhibitions, toys, and much, much more. As Kavanaugh would put it, the kit and caboodle!

Black and White and Read All Over

Kavanaugh is, and always has been, newsworthy. Often featured in both national and trade publications since the early days of her career, she has also written extensively on design. Notably, her 1994 feature for *I.D.* magazine, "A Secret History of Design in Los Angeles" (coauthored with Michael McDonough), brought greater attention to the remarkable contributions of a group of LA designers who had previously been considered part of a general West Coast backwater.

Kavanaugh's achievements have also been recognized in other arenas. Her work was included in four of the twelve legendary *California Design* exhibitions at the Pasadena Art Museum, events that created a national fervor for California craft and design between 1962 and 1976. In 2011 a toy she had prototyped in 1965 was included in the Los Angeles County Museum of Art exhibition *California Design, 1930-1965: "Living in a Modern Way."* Kavanaugh's recent accolades include the Los Angeles Design Festival 2014 Julia Morgan ICON Award, the 2016 American Institute of Graphic Arts (AIGA) Medal, and the 2016 Ladislav Sutnar Prize from the University of West Bohemia in the Czech Republic. ❀ Now, on the eve of her ninetieth birthday, Kavanaugh still contributes frequently to design panels. Even when she's not on the stage, she can generally be found just below, her hand waving, with so much more to say.

" According to Gere, the 'hand' is always better. Inclusivity supersedes exclusivity. Narrow categories and binary thinking give way to her concept that good design can come from a vast number of unexpected sources. Still working, Gere consistently makes great sense to me. How could you not admire a woman who has the bold audacity to carry a rubber chicken purse? "
— Suzanne Isken, Executive Director, Craft and Folk Art Museum

" I met Gere a few years ago at Rosamund Felsen's art gallery, which is a kind of crossroads for meeting interesting people. I have to admit that at the time, I didn't know who Gere was, but somehow she knew who I was. I think she always has her antennae up, sensing what's going on in the world. I remember asking her if she was a graphic designer and she clarified that she designed everything, which I soon understood to be wholeheartedly true. ❀ I think what impresses me most about Gere is that while she inhabits a rarefied world of high design, her approach is far from expressing a dogmatic or singular style. She embodies a strong design aesthetic, yet her art is open to and informed by the tactical circumstances of life. Her force field is variable and multivalent, but somehow it all holds together in a way that can only be described as uniquely Gere Kavanaugh. " — Ken Smith, Ken Smith Workshop

early years

memphis
days

← ← A silkscreened textile (left) and wallpaper (right) were inspired by a hedge in the backyard of Kavanaugh's childhood home. Both were designed while Kavanaugh was at the Memphis Academy of Arts, ca. 1949.

↑↑ Kavanaugh (dressed as a flower) and other students at a Memphis Academy of Arts party, ca. 1951. Her costume was inspired by a Paul Klee painting.

↑ Advertisement for the Memphis Academy of Arts Junior Saturday School, 1950. Kavanaugh attended the school from 1937 until 1951.

→ Kavanaugh, age twenty, while a student at the Memphis Academy of Arts, 1949.

Like a magpie, Kavanaugh gathered ideas from the world around her. The Memphis Zoo, right across the street from her house, was a wonderland for a child with a powerful sense of curiosity and fed a lifelong fascination with nature that would surface regularly in her designs. At home, rare books collected by her father offered another kind of inspiration. On rainy days Kavanaugh would trace or copy images from her father's library, prompting her parents to enroll her in the Memphis Academy of Arts Junior Saturday School in 1937, when she was eight years old. Kavanaugh remained at the Academy until she received her BFA in 1951, and it was there that she was introduced to printing on textiles, a process that would prove central to her future career. Though her parents were supportive of her interest in art, there were limits to what they could imagine. "I don't expect you to do anything with this," her father once said, "but I do expect your life to be enriched." ⁋ But Kavanaugh's undeniable skill and highly original eye were easily recognized, and her exceptional talent in drawing and painting won her a scholarship to graduate school at Parsons School of Design in New York City and a place at Cranbrook Academy of Art in Bloomfield Hills, Michigan, just outside of Detroit. Believing that New York would be "too much," she headed to Cranbrook, an environment she would find both nurturing and stimulating, much like home.

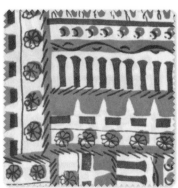

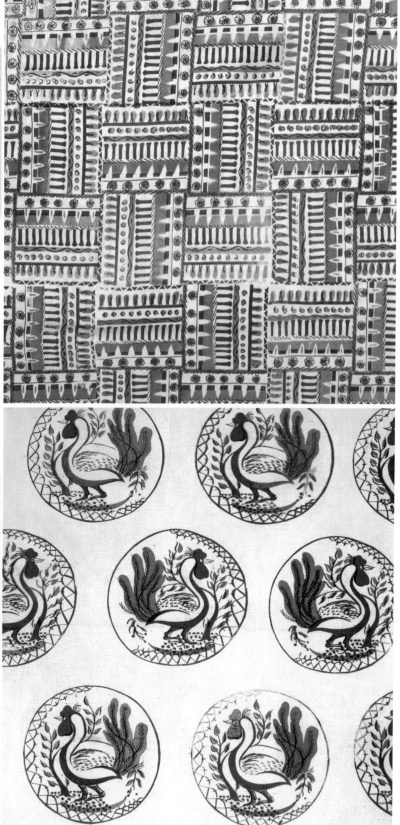

↑→ Textile with a print influenced by a design Kavanaugh discovered in Owen Jones's seminal text, *The Grammar of Ornament*, ca. 1949.

↑→ Silkscreened textile based on Pennsylvania Dutch dinnerware, ca. 1949.

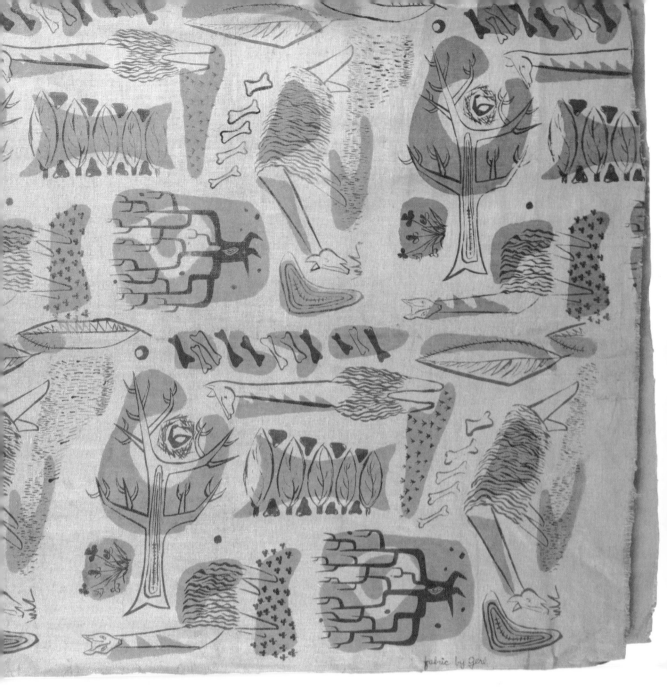

←↑ **ANIMALS AT THE ZOO, CA. 1949.** This silkscreened textile was inspired by Kavanaugh's many childhood visits to the Memphis Zoo.

cranbrook life

↑ Kavanaugh (center, standing), costumed as a football princess for Cranbrook's parody game, the Cranberry Bowl, 1951. The Architecture and Design Departments were pitted against Painting and Sculpture.

→ Kavanaugh (bottom row, third from left) and other Cranbrook students photographed in front of the Eliel Saarinen-designed library, summer 1952. Attendance during the summer was optional, but additional students, sometimes faculty at other institutions, often joined the ranks.

Established in 1932 to promote handsome, thoughtfully crafted goods that reflected an ethically responsible life, Cranbrook Academy of Art went on to cultivate new talent to develop new expressions using modern technologies in areas including ceramics, fiber, metalsmithing, and architecture. The school played an exceptional role in developing the American modern design that reached the international stage in the 1950s and has remained highly influential to this day. ¶ Cranbrook's idyllic and intimate campus provided fertile artistic soil for a small group of students—around 125—whose conviviality appealed to Kavanaugh's irrepressibly social nature. When studios closed at 11 p.m., classmates gathered for spontaneous late-night rendezvous with the architects from the nearby Eero Saarinen and Associates office at a roadside restaurant. Other events, such as costume parties and a football game dubbed the Cranberry Bowl, took more planning. Alongside the fun, however, rigor prevailed. There was no dawdling and dabbling— the unserious were sent packing. A natural explorer with a drive to experiment, Kavanaugh tried everything, applying her artistic sensibility to a range of media including textiles, product design, jewelry, and illustration. ¶ Her funds dwindling, Kavanaugh graduated in 1952 after only fifteen months (instead of the usual two years), becoming the third woman to receive an MFA in Design from Cranbrook. Her thesis project, an installation of furniture, textiles, books, and toys all of her own design, was a harbinger of her prodigious abilities and capacity to integrate craft and design, qualities that would characterize her lengthy career.

28

↓ A curtain of silkscreened textiles served as the backdrop for the diverse elements of Kavanaugh's thesis, among them a rug, table, chair, jewelry, lighting, and toys.

← Designs for textile patterns often started with a silkscreen on paper, as seen on the far left. The printed textile on the right appeared in Kavanaugh's thesis exhibition.

← Two colorways of a pattern with onion-like forms. For the black-and-white version, Kavanaugh hand-painted an area gray to provide a surprising deviation.

←← When Kavanaugh wanted to silkscreen metallic gold ink onto fabric, she was met with skepticism by one member of the faculty. But the willful young designer plowed ahead, and the results proved her naysayer wrong.

← Kavanaugh offset the same abstract tree pattern and printed it in two colors to achieve a richer, more textured effect. At Cranbrook she learned various printing processes and experimented with silkscreening in particular.

Cranbrook Graduate Thesis Exhibition, 1952

At Cranbrook Kavanaugh's passion for textiles was stoked by exceptional teachers and fellow students. Marianne Strengell, head of the Department of Weaving and Textile Design, and weaver Jack Lenor Larsen, who graduated a year before Kavanaugh, were just two of the stellar talents she encountered in the 1950s at the school, which had produced such luminaries of modern design as Ray Eames, Florence Knoll, and Ruth Adler Schnee, among many others.

For her thesis project Kavanaugh designed a side table with a metal-rod base and wood and Formica trays that could be slipped out and rotated. She wrote in the accompanying notes, "Designed as a fun table. One to be used when the occasion for an extra table is in need – such as a party or extra company. It can easily be folded and stored away."

Kavanaugh posing in a chair she designed as part of her thesis project. The chair comprised a metal base and canvas sling with a seat cushion covered in fabric she had silkscreened. In her notes she wrote, "A very comfortable chair – light in weight – easy to move around – can fit in any setting according to the material used – easy to produce."

↑ RIDDLE RIDDLE, CA. 1951. Kavanaugh experimented with the way a narrative might unfold visually by adding flaps revealing surprises in the gouache-and-ink illustrations beneath.

← MY APPLE TREE, CA. 1952.
This book, which relates the
seasonal experiences of a tree,
was also part of Kavanaugh's
thesis project. The story was
cut and glued into rectangles
on the left-hand pages.
Over the years the type has
become unstuck and fallen
into the gutter. Kavanaugh
sent the book to Doubleday &
Company, but unfortunately the
submission was not successful.

Cranbrook Illustrated Book Projects, 1951–52

Combining her love of drawing, animals, and nature
with the Southern tradition of storytelling,
Kavanaugh created several books with gouache and ink
illustrations while studying at Cranbrook. Each was
unique and hand-bound.

34

As the sapling in *My Apple Tree* grows, so does the space required to contain its expanding branches and foliage. Pages fold out, doubling and quadrupling as the tree transforms. Kavanaugh's charming illustrations depict the tree's joyful interactions with a young girl and a flock of colorful birds across the seasons.

general motors

FEMININE AUTO SHOW, 1958.
Inside the General Motors
Technical Center, flame-
colored nylon chiffon banners
were draped from the top of
the dome in a dramatic gesture
that filled the space.

Kavanaugh's first job, at General Motors, resulted
from the strong connection between Cranbrook and
GM, whose facilities in Warren, Michigan, had been
designed by Eero Saarinen. Saarinen's father, Eliel,
had been the architect of Cranbrook's campus and had
acted as the Academy of Art's founding president. In
1952 she joined the Styling Division under GM Vice
President Harley Earl. Already known for his visionary
automotive designs, Earl cemented his maverick reputa-
tion by hiring a group of women for a team GM marketed
as the "Damsels of Design." Most of the damsels—all
highly accomplished in their field, despite the dep-
recating nickname—held the title of stylist and were
tasked with designing car interiors. Kavanaugh, who
was responsible for GM trade shows, kitchen interior
models, and various other projects, was recognized
with the title of designer. ¶ The ultimate showcase for
GM's products envisioned "by ladies, for ladies" was
its 1958 Feminine Auto Show, staged in GM's landmark
Eero Saarinen-designed Technical Center, which had
opened just two years earlier. The show featured cars
with special details such as vanities; umbrella holders; and smooth, rounded surfaces meant to prevent
nylon snags. ¶ Kavanaugh created arresting settings
for the model cars, as well as displays for GM's
Frigidaire division, to show how the products might be
used. Working among creatives that included not only
Earl but also architect and interior designer Warren
Platner and industrial designer-educators Rowena Reed
Kostellow and Alexander Kostellow provided an environment for Kavanaugh in which she could channel the
liberated experimentation of her time at Cranbrook into
exuberant but refined applications for GM. Kavanaugh
was at GM for a total of five years, from 1952 to 1954
and 1955 to 1958. General Motors gave her solid ground
to bloom into the designer she would become.

For the Feminine Auto Show, Kavanaugh—pictured with two Oldsmobile models styled by fellow Damsel Peggy Sauer—had a French garden party in mind. She created thirty-foot-tall net towers designed to contain one hundred rented canaries. "When the lights were turned on the birds started singing," says Kavanaugh. "Only one got out; we returned ninety-nine." Enthusiastic press coverage noted that "colored cellophane under the plastic floors of the cages gave rainbow hues," much to the winged creatures' delight.

↑ MOTORAMA, 1954. The floor display was likely designed by LeRoy Kiefer, GM's director of product and exhibit designs. It shared the futuristic starburst motif with promotional mock-ups designed by Kavanaugh, shown above.

↑ Vice President of Styling Harley Earl and "dream cars" in front of the Styling Auditorium at the General Motors Technical Center in Warren, Michigan, 1956.

← Two trade displays from around 1959 showcasing textiles for car interiors. The displays took place in "The Dome," as Kavanaugh referred to the Exhibition Center that was part of the GM campus. The upside-down, bowl-shaped space presented a design challenge to which Kavanaugh responded by creating dramatic sculptural elements.

Trade Show Displays, late 1950s

Kavanaugh solved the design challenge posed by the cavernous domed space by creating dramatic, towering sculptural elements in lightweight materials.

↑ Kavanaugh's kitchen design features Frigidaire appliances surrounded by thoughtful touches direct from her own hand. These include the gray-and-white floral curtains at left and the charming illustration of food-storage shelving nested between stacked ovens and the refrigerator.

Frigidaire Kitchen Designs, 1954–57

Among Kavanaugh's myriad responsibilities at General Motors was the creation of displays for the company's Frigidaire appliance division. As part of a small team, Kavanaugh designed modern model kitchens that show-cased GM's refrigerators, stove tops, and ovens that were integrated into the cabinetry rather than free-standing. Her interiors included an array of clever, forward-thinking approaches such as ease-of-cooking workflow or the ability to entertain *while* preparing a meal. Her attention to details conveyed each kitchen's unique concept, from the cabinetry down to the fruit bowls, flower arrangements, or potted plants that were placed artfully on tabletops and counters.

glass holder

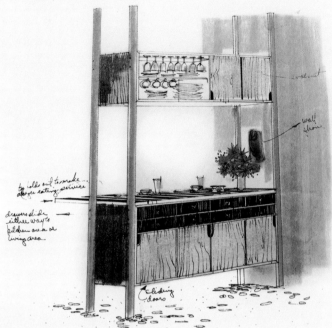

These sketches from 1956–57 illustrate Kavanaugh's concept for a "dream kitchen" commissioned by Harley Earl to "meet the needs of the 'bachelor girl.'" Features of the unit sketched at left include a foldout table, drawers that opened on either side, and a wall-mounted telephone. In the unit sketched below, appliances are concealed below the counter. Her ideas reflected an ideal entertaining space for the young, single woman, like Kavanaugh herself.

top folds out to make larger eating service

drawers slide either way to kitchen area or living area

wall phone

walnut

sliding doors

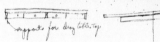

supports for drop table top

Kitchen Stg between dining & 'kitchen area

(Mechanical Core)

fridge   disposal   dishwasher   oven

↑ Visible in this 1957 GM press photograph are Damsels of Design (clockwise from top left) Gere Kavanaugh, Dagmar Arnold, Jan Krebs, and Peggy Sauer.

→ May 26, 1956, General Motors press release and photograph.

General Motors, "Damsels Of Design," 1955–58

In 1956 GM began to highlight a group of female designers working at GM Styling and dubbed them the Damsels of Design. Harley Earl encouraged the recruitment of women into design, in part to position GM as a forward-thinking company but also to appeal directly to women, who had an increasing influence on automotive purchases. The Damsels worked at GM until 1958, when Earl retired and his replacement deemed the women a distraction. After leaving GM, many had successful careers as industrial designers.

FOR RELEASE SUNDAY, MAY 26

DAMSELS OF DESIGN -- These talented General Motors women designers are allowing women, who today cast the deciding vote in the purchase of seven out of ten cars, to actually help design automobiles, Harley J. Earl, GM Vice President in charge of Styling, declared Saturday. Mr. Earl, shown here explaining a model futuristic car to his feminine stylists, said the use of women to help design GM cars and appliances has been very successful. Seated is Sandra Longyear, of Manhasset, N.Y. Standing (1 to r) are Dagmar Arnold, Glen Cove, N.Y.; Jayne Van Alstyne, East Lansing, Mich.; Jan Krebs, Waterbury, Conn.; Gere Kavanaugh, Detroit, Mich.; Peggy Sauer, Detroit, Mich.; and Helene Pollins, Far Rockaway, N.Y. Two other GM women designers were on vacation when this photo was taken.

VARIATION ON A THEME, MID–1950s.
Kavanaugh designed this mixed-media mural installation composed of elements in lacquer, steel, and fabric as part of the styling group's executive office areas in the Styling Building at the GM Technical Center.

❝ In 2010 I invited Gere Kavanaugh to the General Motors Technical Center campus to interview her for a lecture I was giving on the history of women in design at GM. It was her first return visit after over fifty years. This very important mid-century modern architectural site, designed by Eero Saarinen, was brand new when Gere began working there; it visually and metaphorically represented the unabashed optimism of the future of American industry in the mid-1950s. ❄ Gere was one of a small group recruited by GM as the first women designers in the automotive industry. The legendary vice president of styling, Harley Earl, understood the importance of women's influence in the purchasing of cars and sought out their voice in the design process. I have had the extraordinary privilege to interview a number of these women, and they all have a certain reverence for the design opportunity that they were given at a time when they were the 'firsts.' None of them wanted to dwell or focus on whatever inequalities they may have encountered. All of them took the opportunity like a gift from heaven, learned everything they could from the experience, and went on to interesting and fulfilling careers in all areas of design. ❄ Ms. Kavanaugh's path is certainly indicative of this.**❞** – Susan Skarsgard, Designer Manager, GM Design Archive and Special Collections

Decorator Sets Off Cars

By Jessie Ash Arndt

Woman's Editor of
The Christian Science Monitor

Detroit

When General Motors Corporation unveiled the cars whose interiors were done by its nine "Damsels of Design" this spring, it also called on one of its damsel designers to dream up the setting for the glamorous unveiling.

The young woman responsible for this was "Gere" Kavanaugh, who hails originally from Memphis, and studied at the Memphis Academy of Art, but who came north to attend Cranbrook Academy of Art, Bloomfield Hills, Mich., to major in design.

When she had finished at Cranbrook she applied to General Motors and was employed. After two years she went for a year to Victor Gruen, a Detroit design firm, and then was asked to return to General Motors two years ago. She is in the design group at the General Design Studio, associated with three men designers.

General Motors

Gere Kavanaugh

Bird-Cage Theme

They do all architectural interiors and special exhibits. These included last summer's exhibit of automotive fabrics which was held in the Auditorium of Styling at the General Motors Technical Center, in Warren, Mich., outside of Detroit.

This was also the scene of this year's spring showing of cars by the ladies for the ladies. With the idea of a French garden party in mind, Miss Kavanaugh found she needed birds and flowers. She ordered three cages 30 feet high, 2 feet 10 inches in diameter, made of Swiss cotton net fastened just like a dress, with hooks and eyes at the openings.

A chain was hung down the center of each cage, with wooden dowels, ¾-inch in diameter, spaced at intervals from top to bottom as perches. Colored cellophane under the plastic floors of the cages gave rainbow hues which apparently were as pleasing to the birds as to the visitors, for they sang and winged their way up and down in their floor-to-ceiling enclosures as though they had all outdoors to fly in.

Outdoor Effects

The 90 birds housed there were rented. So were the blooming white hyacinth plants which circled the auditorium and marked off what looked like tiled terraces where the cars stood. The "tiles" were contact paper ones, which adhered neatly to the auditorium floor. Miss Kavanaugh dislikes carpets or rugs as a base for the display of cars "for, naturally, they belong in an outdoor setting."

She used nylon chiffon — a feminine type of material, she noted—in orange and flame color as banners from the ceiling to the light cove.

The total effect was gay, airy, and one of song and fragrance—and the remarkable feature of the setting was that, except for the canaries, it could all be gathered up and transported in the back of one station wagon!

Fun on the Side

Miss Kavanaugh last year digressed long enough from the field of industrial design to decorate the handsome new home of Anthony de Lorenzo, General Motors vice-president in charge of public relations, in Flint, Mich. Mr. and Mrs. de Lorenzo have four children. Their house is ranch style, with a huge living room, four bedrooms, a large sun room, a family room. In the basement are a big playroom and game room as well as a laundry and a tool shop claimed exclusively by Mr. de Lorenzo and his son.

Miss Kavanaugh used Alexander Girard wallpapers in the bedroom for the two daughters, in the hall and the kitchen. The paper has geometric designs, but doesn't look "designed," she says. "It looks as though it just grew there. In fact, the whole house has a lived-in look.".

In furniture, she chose Finn Juhl, Hans Wegner, Charlie Eames, and George Nelson designs, which contributed to a "folksy" feeling. She selected simple dinnerware and stainless steel for the dining-room service.

One bathroom has pearlscent Naughahyde—an automotive fabric—with a beige print and another glazed bronze tiles. In this she also used contemporary Danish hanging lamps. For both, she selected orange towels—for she did the house from the largest to the smallest interior detail.

With her mother, Mrs. Bernadette Kavanaugh, Miss Kavanaugh lives in an apartment where she has combined modern and traditional pieces.

She has recently designed a line of fabrics outside her regular job, for a New York firm. She likes to cook, sail, and ski, but often her recreation keeps her right in her favorite artistic groove. She does painting in tempora casein and prints wall hangings when she finds time. Music is also one of her delights, although she says a little ruefully, "But I don't perform."

Article by Jessie Ash Arndt, *Christian Science Monitor*, May 14, 1958. This piece appeared in syndicate in various newspapers across the country.

victor gruen
associates

↑ A playful moment between Kavanaugh and her mentor Rudi Baumfeld captured in 1968. Baumfeld called her his "daughter by choice."

From 1954-55, during a brief respite from General Motors, Kavanaugh worked in the Detroit office of the Los Angeles-based architecture and planning firm Victor Gruen Associates. She returned to GM from 1955 to 1958, after which she pursued independent projects until she was approached, in 1959, by both Gruen Associates and Eero Saarinen and Associates. To choose between the two offers, Kavanaugh planned a weeklong trip to the West Coast. While in Los Angeles, she paid a visit to the progressive Immaculate Heart College and Sisters Corita Kent and Magdalen Mary, artist-activist nuns whom she had met in Memphis. Greeting her at the school, Kavanaugh recalls, Magdalen Mary exclaimed, "Hello! How are you? You must have a job out here! We have a house for you!" She decided to stay. ¶ Gruen Associates specialized in department stores but became legendary—some would say notorious—for conceiving and realizing the massive suburban shopping centers that appeared in postwar America. From 1960 until she struck out on her own in 1964, Kavanaugh was director of interiors at the Los Angeles office under partner Rudi Baumfeld. There she met young architects Frank Gehry and Greg Walsh. The three developed a close bond while collaborating on many projects, including designs for the Joseph Magnin Company, a chain of trend-setting specialty stores. Kavanaugh departed from Gruen's office in 1964.

Ladies' Lounge, Wieboldt's Department Store, Chicago, Illinois, 1961

Designed by Kavanaugh, the red, pink, maroon, and gold mosaic covering the walls and ceiling was fabricated by Chicago artist Ada Korsakaite.

↑ In the capsules, scenes with animatronic puppets designed by Jan Steward represent (from left) the United States, Thailand, and Puerto Rico.

↑ Midtown Plaza.

→ Clock of the Nations holds center stage in the Midtown Plaza mall, mid–late 1970s.

Clock of the Nations, Midtown Plaza, Rochester, New York, 1961

Activating the cavernous atrium of Rochester's Midtown Plaza mall (a project developed by a Gruen Associates team that included Gehry and Walsh), the twenty-eight-foot-tall Clock of the Nations, designed by Kavanaugh, nodded to traditional clock towers while adding whimsy to the shopping center. Every day at noon, the twelve capsules surrounding the central tower would open and rotate, revealing scenes with animatronic puppets representing world cultures.

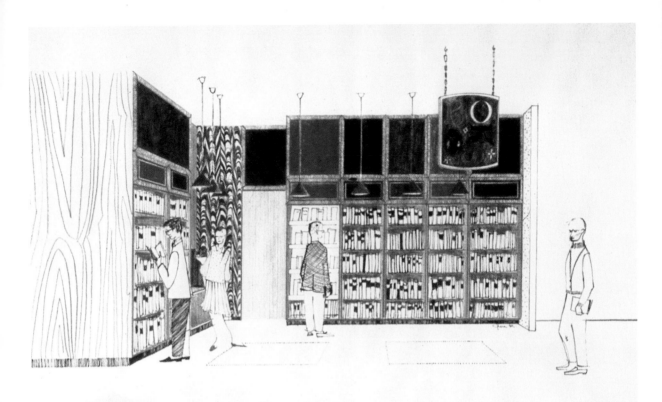

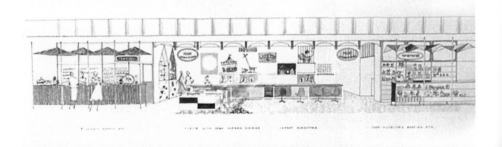

Department store presentation
drawings created in the early
1960s. Kavanaugh likely
completed this series for the
May Company department store
in University Heights, Ohio.

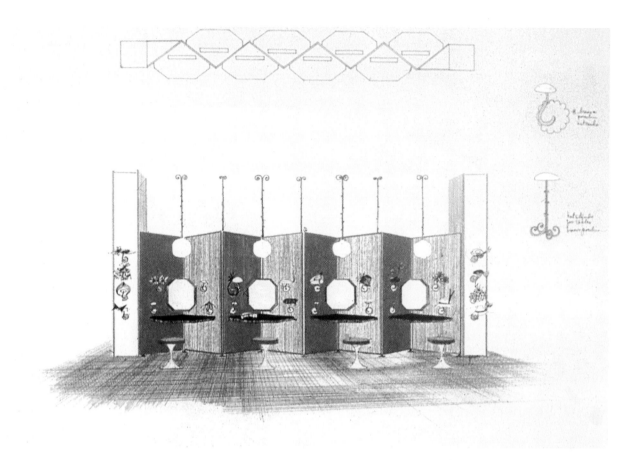

Department store
presentation
drawings created in
the early 1960s.

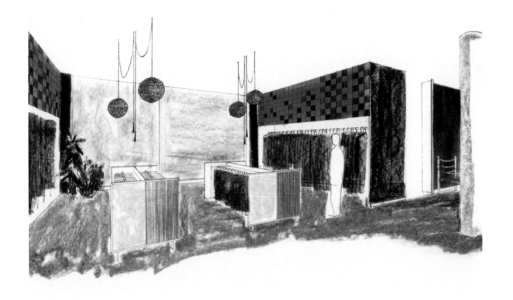

men's wear

men's shirts

" Upon graduation from Cranbrook Academy of Art in 1952, Gere Kavanaugh wrote about the interconnected nature of the world and of design, noting that: 'Design is vital and organic. It is a living thing.... Design is all around us. Every hour that you are awake or asleep you are in contact with it. The field itself must be living or otherwise it will become stagnant.' This statement would not be unusual for Academy of Art students like Gere to write, as it reflects the subtle influences of Cranbrook itself. Cranbrook was and is a holistic experience, designed by the noted Finnish architect Eliel Saarinen, where he created a Gesamtkunstwerk, a total work of art. Saarinen believed the role of the designer operated at every scale: from the design of the flatware, to the table it was placed on, to the chair where one would sit, to the room where these objects would live, to the architecture of the house, to the adjoining landscape and gardens, and to the neighborhood and finally to the city itself. This founding philosophy was ingrained in its earliest graduates, particularly its architects and designers. Gere Kavanaugh embodies this ideology. ❀ Cranbrook's hothouse environment of artistic experimentation essentially birthed the modernist design movement of mid-twentieth-century America, with designers such as Charles and Ray Eames, Florence Knoll, Harry Bertoia, Ruth Adler Schnee, Jack Lenor Larsen, and

Eero Saarinen, among many others. The 'living quality' of design that Gere wrote about can be interpreted as both an expression of living with design and the very act of designing itself. For many graduates, it was ultimately about designing one's life. ✿ That sense of restless experimentation would resonate throughout her distinguished career, long after those early days in Michigan. She also presciently warned that a designer 'could lose his vitality and vigor by specializing.' Taking this as a form of career advice, Gere's varied design practice – textiles, graphics, interiors, furniture – resists compartmentalization, and that approach is quintessentially Cranbrook. Fueled by an innate curiosity of the world around her, Gere's concluding thoughts are as apropos today as they were sixty-four years ago: 'Design is an accumulation of everything that you perceive. It is all taken in, chewed and digested and stored for a future time. When the proper time comes an idea is born of this. Ideas don't just spring from out of nowhere, but from an accumulation of things and impressions.' Gere has never stopped looking – and her ideas and her designs keep coming. 𝕁 – Andrew Blauvelt, Director, Cranbrook Art Museum, and Christopher Scoates, former Director, Cranbrook Academy of Art and Art Museum

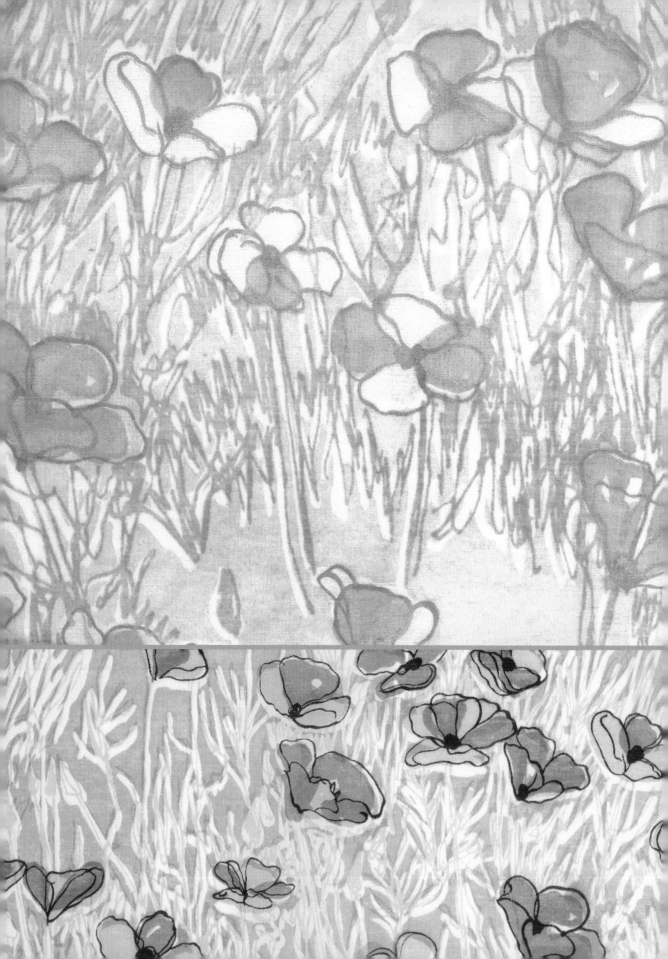

gere kavanaugh/
designs

Excerpt from *Architecture/West*, mid-1960s.

Marvin Rand photos

Where the Architects Hang Their Hats

BLACK AND WHITE PHOTOS can't do it justice. Squint your eyes a bit and imagine the dark purple doors, with yellow and green walls clearly visible clear to the landing. Progress upwards and see the vast white ceilinged, white walled loft space, trimmed in dark brown fir and natural redwood, with a great orange and yellow striped curtain that is the focal point of the drafting room and conceals—of all things—the coat closet.

No loft space ever had it so good, including the freshly stripped and polished maple floor, all so simply and economically effective. Partitions are Celotex, for acoustic purposes and also to provide plenty of pin-up space for still more color in drawings and in paintings by local artists.

This is the "home" of Frank O. Gehry and C. Gregory Walsh Jr.; architects and of Gere Kavanaugh, designer. The office is involved in architecture, city planning and interior design, currently working on a master plan for Newburgh, New York, and a multi-story office building in Beverly Hills. Their Kay Jewelers office was featured in the September 1964 issue of A/W. Gehry was graduated from USC and continued education at the Harvard Graduate School. He was associated with Victor Gruen and Andre Remondet, Paris architect. Walsh is another USC-Gruen man who also worked with Welton Becket & Associates.

GEHRY and WALSH • Los Angeles

One of the Fairchild Business Newspapers

Women's Wear Daily

THE RETAILER'S DAILY NEWSPAPER ®

Vol. 110 No. 3 ★ ★   NEW YORK, N. Y., WEDNESDAY, JANUARY 6, 1965   TEN CENTS   One Year $18 Payable in Advance

GERE KAVANAUGH . . . YOUNG AND VERY MUCH WITH IT . . . a designer in the contemporary mood . . . specializing in home and store interiors, providing her customers with "a way to live within our time."

Joseph Magnin's customers probably wouldn't recognize her name, but she's responsible for the fun and high-fashion mood of many of the J. Magnin stores that reflects so well the type of merchandise the store specializes in.

GERE sees the J. Magnin customer as one who enjoys a "bizaz type of living," who would rather indulge herself in chic fur fashions than the chic chic (which often borders on dowdy chic, according to Geré).

THE SETTING FOR MERCHANDISE AND CUSTOMER is designed for the present . . . no pseudo elegance, no borrowing from the past. Her interiors create their own "elegance of the present time" with quality craftmanship and design integrity.

For example, in one of the newest J. Magnin stores (her sketches above) at Santa Rosa, she used linen panels of crewel embroidery in flower garden colors over the doorway . . . the chandelier in the gown shop is covered with white porcelain roses . . . The floor is carpeted in salt and pepper tweed, the departments defined by bright insets of color — red for the gown shop, orange for the sportswear, and yellow for the shoe section (yellow seems to set off medium and dark-tone shoes to advantage).

Sap-grain cherry and walnut were used for display fixtures, the prominent grain providing the warmth and quality of wood to the selling floor.

THE TOPANGA PLAZA STORE was a bit of an experiment, the high-fashion look toned down just a bit, the accent still on fun chic in deference to the more casual way of life in the San Fernando Valley. Yet the contemporary elegant touches are still there . . . a giant tapestry on one wall and a large metal sculpture in the gown shop. A black and white checked carpet was a bright idea that didn't quite work (in large expanses all those checks produce a disturbing optical illusion) . . . so it was replaced with a gay fun floral in sunny tones of orange, yellow, white and coral.

A DESIGNER CAN'T BE EXPOSED to all those women's fashions without getting ideas of her own. And Geré fairly bubbles with ideas. She designs many of her own clothes, and her mother, a former professional seamstress, makes them for her.

Her favorite designers . . . Adele Simpson ("Her clothes are kind of timely and you don't see too much of her things in the magazines.") . . . Sybil Connolly ("Great, elegant country clothes, on-the-go clothes, also very timely.")

This spring, J. Magnin will be selling a canvas tote bag (above) with a bright floral motif designed by Geré and made by Mr. Chips.

GERE'S INFLUENCE is not confined to California. She has designed ZCMI's new packaging. And when she was working for Victor Gruen, she did a spectacular powder room for Wieboldt's, Chicago. Overseas, the N K department store in Sweden has just ordered her gay floral placemats (above) also carried by J. Magnin.

STORES, RESTAURANTS, PRIVATE HOMES, GRAPHICS, FASHION, FURNITURE . . . just name it and Gere's got a million ideas on how it can be done.

—SHIRLEY PLOTKIN,
Los Angeles Bureau

Photos by Nick Ackerman

joseph magnin

The Joseph Magnin Company was a predominately California-based chain of high-end specialty stores founded in San Francisco and widely credited with cultivating the "California Cool" look of the 1960s. Kavanaugh put it best when she described the store's customer for *Women's Wear Daily* as "one who enjoys the bizaz type of living, who would rather indulge herself in the chic fun fashion than the chic chic (which often borders on the dowdy chic)." ¶ Kavanaugh began working with Joseph Magnin when she joined the Los Angeles office of Victor Gruen Associates in 1960. After less than a year with the firm, she was assigned by Rudi Baumfeld to design elements of this prized client's revamp of their store located at Stockton and O'Farrell Streets in the heart of San Francisco. Kavanaugh traveled to the corporate offices and so impressed company executives Ellen Magnin Newman (Joseph Magnin's granddaughter) and her husband, Walter Newman, that they requested Kavanaugh's assistance with a nearby property at the corner of Montgomery and Bush Streets. ¶ Kavanaugh's relationship with Joseph Magnin and the Newmans continued after she left Gruen in 1964 to establish her own firm, Gere Kavanaugh/Designs, in a studio she shared with her friend and former colleague Frank Gehry and his partner, Greg Walsh. When Gehry won the commission to design a new Joseph Magnin store for South Coast Plaza in Costa Mesa, California, he asked Kavanaugh to work with him on the store's interiors, while their studio mate, graphic designer Deborah Sussman, created signage and other graphic elements. ¶ Kavanaugh designed interiors for eight Joseph Magnin stores across California, including three locations in San Francisco and one each in Mountain View, Santa Rosa, Sherman Oaks, Costa Mesa, and Topanga Canyon. Her program for each location was unique and comprehensive, encompassing everything from the overall color scheme to the materials, lighting, display fixtures, furnishings, carpets, and wall treatments.

↑→ Rudi Baumfeld's black-and-white sketches for the remodeling of the second floor of Joseph Magnin's main San Francisco location were brought to life by Kavanaugh's brilliant eye for color.

←←← POPPIES, CA. 1960s. Inspired by the Californian poppies that bloom every spring, Kavanaugh designed this pattern for C. W. Stockwell as both a fabric and a wallpaper. The yellow and orange colorway was used in the bedroom set in the 1968 film *Rosemary's Baby*.

Stockton & O'Farrell, San Francisco, 1960

Montgomery and Bush,
San Francisco, 1960

←← Kavanaugh's idea to adorn the facade of the Financial District store with blue Mexican glass tiles was considered outrageous. According to Ellen Magnin Newman, it took her father, Cyril Magnin, months of negotiation to convince city officials. However, once built, it was immediately clear that Kavanaugh's idea had been brilliant – everyone knew exactly where to find the store.

← Kavanaugh commissioned Ruth Asawa to create wire sculptures to hang inside the store. While most department stores were decorated with "big, swoopy" chandeliers, Kavanaugh understood that Asawa's artworks would make a far more dramatic impression.

Coddingtown Mall,
Santa Rosa, 1964

←↑ For this Joseph Magnin location, Kavanaugh created a visual smorgasbord. Each department in the store was demarcated by a different color – yellow for shoes and red for gowns.

Kavanaugh in front of
a carpet she designed
for Joseph Magnin's
Topanga Canyon
location, which opened
in 1964.

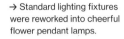
→ Standard lighting fixtures were reworked into cheerful flower pendant lamps.

↑ Flowers, flowers, everywhere! Kavanaugh designed "the whole everything" for the Joseph Magnin store in Mountain View, from the metallic flowered wallpapers produced for Bill Keliehor to supersized daisies that covered the floor. She took this project on after her time at Gruen Associates, having established Gere Kavanaugh/Designs in 1964. Kavanaugh considers Mountain View the apotheosis of her design work for Joseph Magnin.

**Mayfield Mall,
Mountain View, 1966**

← Orange and yellow acrylic flower petals transform this hanging light fixture.

↑→ Supergraphics featuring the poppy, the California state flower, adorn a stairwell. Chrome accents complement circular wall and floor tiles, while a bright yellow zinnia clock adds another floral moment.

↑→ Bold banners identified each department, and cheerful details such as a bright yellow clock and cobalt blue tiles made the Mayfield Mall Joseph Magnin store exciting and playful from every angle.

Sherman Oaks, 1966

↑ For the Joseph Magnin
store in Fox Plaza, Kavanaugh
created a riot of colors.

**Fox Plaza,
San Francisco, 1966**

→ Kavanaugh based the design of her collapsible, square Market Umbrella — used to create intimate spaces in the store's Soupçon restaurant — on umbrellas she had seen in Mexico. At Gehry's request that the wallcoverings feel like clouds, she worked with Sister Corita Kent's students from Immaculate Heart College to create a joyful and buoyant design.

← Kavanaugh, hired by Frank Gehry to design the interiors, furnished the women's salon with sofas by George Kasparian upholstered in fabric by Jack Lenor Larsen.

South Coast Plaza, Costa Mesa, 1968

↑ Sweet daisy stools and hangings adorned each dressing room.

→ Kavanaugh designed these chairs specifically for the South Coast Plaza store. They were designed to be grouped together.

One of the Fairchild Business Newspapers

Home Furnishings Daily.

TEN CENTS

One Year $12
Payable in Advance

Printed in U.S.A.

NEW YORK, N. Y., TUESDAY, JULY 2, 1968

Vol. 40   No. 129   ★ ★ ★

CONTRACT

CLEAN, GRAPHIC, TODAY.

It's Joseph Magnin's new store in Costa Mesa, Calif., where architect Frank Gehry has recreated in 1968 terms his vision of H. G. Wells' film of the 30s, "Things to Come."

THINGS TO COME ... NOW is alive and fresh.

One of the fresh notes; Sister Mary Corita's graphics — blazoned on the [...] of the store's lunch [...]
See Pages 6 and 7

THINGS TO COME ... NOW

CYRIL MAGNIN CALLS IT EARLY 21ST CENTURY . . . ARCHITECT FRANK GEHRY CALLS IT AN UPDATED VERSION OF "THINGS TO COME," THE H. G. WELLS FILM OF THE THIRTIES . . . DESIGNER GERE KAVANAUGH SIMPLY CALLS IT "NOW."

The Joseph Magnin store in Costa Mesa, Calif., is all of these. Crisp, clean, bold. Strong jewel-like colors create a pleasant environment for merchandising. Total environment decor.

"It's silly seduction to use make-believe architecture, such as English Tudor," Miss Kavanaugh says. "This is alive and fresh. The Magnins are very savvy people in trying to create a new environment. They realize that everything is of today and the time is now. It's exciting for a person to work on it. You just let your imagination go."

This is the first department store designed by Gehry, who also did the Marjorie Merriwether Post Music Pavilion in Washington. "We all worked together and gave each other emotional support," he said, referring to the Magnin-Kavanaugh-Gehry entente.

Gehry experimented with lighting.

"The usual store is a static type of thing. But fashion isn't static. It's fickle and changeable. That's why we designed the all-hidden lighting system. We used industrial lighting and it was cheap. BULB COLORS CAN BE CHANGED, SO THAT THE WHOLE STORE CAN BE MADE PINK FOR VALENTINE'S DAY.

"We also have changeable graphics. We felt the display department can change the entire character of the store by change in lighting and graphics. The elevator is designed like a billboard; it has removable panels. The ceiling is totally clean. This is something I insisted on, for it gives a frame for the merchandise. You can see the difference when you go to other stores."

Gehry explains the distractions of hardware in other stores, the equipment or the ceiling being of the same scale as the merchandise on the floor. "We created one great big strong thing."

He admits the lighting experiment didn't work thoroughly, for there are some spots on the ceiling with shadow. "But I'll perfect it in the store I'm doing for the Almaden Center."

Gere Kavanaugh said the colors are slightly offbeat. "They a r e strong pigmented colors which kick off an exciting dimension. It's taken years to get color pigment to be this strong. It was the same way in fashion. The reason for subtle colors in the past was they couldn't get them strong."

The $1 million 40,000-square-foot jewel at South Coat Plaza shopping center is part of JM's new dedication to design.

Already the center of much conjectural anticipation is JM's store at Bullock's Fashion Square in La Habra, which will open Aug. 10.

"THE COSTA MESA STORE IS EARLY 21ST CENTURY," CYRIL MAGNIN SAYS. "LE HABRA WILL PUT US RIGHT INTO THE MIDDLE OF THAT CENTURY."

HECTOR ARCE
—Los Angeles Bureau

CONTRACT

Photos by Marvin Rand

Excerpt from article by Hector Acre, "Things to come....now," *Home Furnishings Daily*, Tuesday, July 2, 1968.

❝ It was Joseph Magnin that brought Gere Kavanaugh into my life, and where I had the good fortune to work closely with her on several projects. One of the outstanding examples of her creative solutions to design challenges was the design of the Joseph Magnin Financial District store on Montgomery Street in San Francisco. The equivalent would have been to put a women's specialty store on Wall Street in the '60s! ❀ The property on which the Joseph Magnin store was to be developed belonged to the very conservative Crocker Land Company. They were stunned and ready to cancel the lease on the building when they saw that Gere was going to put bright blue ceramic tiles in a large mosaic to cover the exterior of the building. Cyril Magnin fought for Gere and ultimately convinced the Crocker Land Company it was the right thing to do. ❀ The interior of the store was a great problem. It was U-shaped to accommodate the entrance to the Crocker Building. To ensure that customers would move through the store from the entrance, Gere hung six wire sculptures by the then-unknown artist Ruth Asawa. People would enter the space, look up to see one sculpture, and continue through the space as the remaining five sculptures drew them through it. Those six sculptures now hang at the entrance of the de Young Museum's tower in San Francisco. **"** — Ellen Magnin Newman, longtime head of Joseph Magnin stores

textiles & paper

Kavanaugh began printing textiles and wallcoverings as a young art student in Memphis. Her passion for pattern and color and for learning new techniques would endure throughout her career. Certainly it was encouraged by her faculty at Cranbrook, where a love affair with textile design was embedded in its tradition of experimentation. In this environment, Kavanaugh was saturated with inspiration. ⁋ Shortly after graduating from Cranbrook, and while she was working for General Motors in Detroit, Kavanaugh designed textiles for Isabel Scott Fabrics. Over the years her relationship with the company expanded into diverse projects, including the design of various promotional materials. Most significantly, in 1968 she helped establish a factory in South Korea, working with the facility on the production of woven silk textiles of her own design that would appeal to American tastes. ⁋ "Color really hit me when I moved to California," Kavanaugh said of her relocation from Detroit to Los Angeles, where in 1972 she launched her own line of brightly patterned textiles, Geraldine Fabrics. ⁋ The 1970s was a fruitful decade for Kavanaugh's wallcovering and paper designs. In a follow-up to the playful wallpaper designs of her early school years, she created stenciled and silkscreened wallcoverings for manufacturers Bill Keliehor Designs and Bob Mitchell Designs and used the wallpapers in some of her own interior design projects, such as Joseph Magnin stores. They were included in the Pasadena Art Museum's famed *California Design* exhibitions, which put handmade and manufactured West Coast design on the national stage. Kavanaugh wrapped up the decade with a collection of metallic wrapping papers for CPS Industries.

→ In a photo taken for the *Los Angeles Times Home* magazine in 1967, Kavanaugh is surrounded by her colorful fabric designs. From left: metallic floral wallpaper produced by Bob Keliehor; The Seasons, designed for Isabel Scott Fabrics; Dots and Triangles wallpaper produced by Bob Mitchell; and paper cutouts used to develop the ikat textiles for Isabel Scott Fabrics. On the loom is a swatch of Crystals for Isabel Scott Fabrics. The tile at Kavanaugh's feet and the floral rug are also her designs.

← Kavanaugh in 1951, her senior year, with her Memphis Academy of Arts classmates, wearing a linoleum block–print textile skirt of her own design.

Various Pattern Designs, late 1940s – early 1970s

↑→ Gaskets and auto parts make up the pattern of this groovy textile that Kavanaugh designed around 1949, while still a student. Kavanaugh was commissioned by Kenneth Kimbrough – a major Memphis society decorator – to produce this fabric for the owner of an auto dealership who wanted all the parts sold through his distributorship incorporated into the design of drapes. It was Kavanaugh's first professional job.

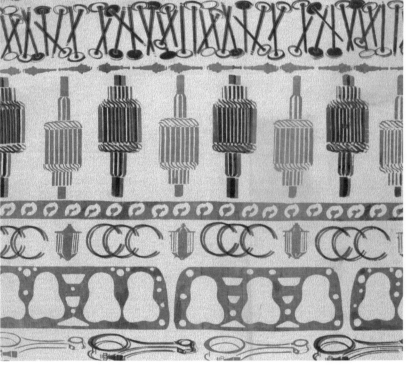

↑→ Kavanaugh made the pattern on this fabric by hand-printing cotton with carved blocks of linoleum at the Memphis Academy of Arts in the late 1940s or early 1950s.

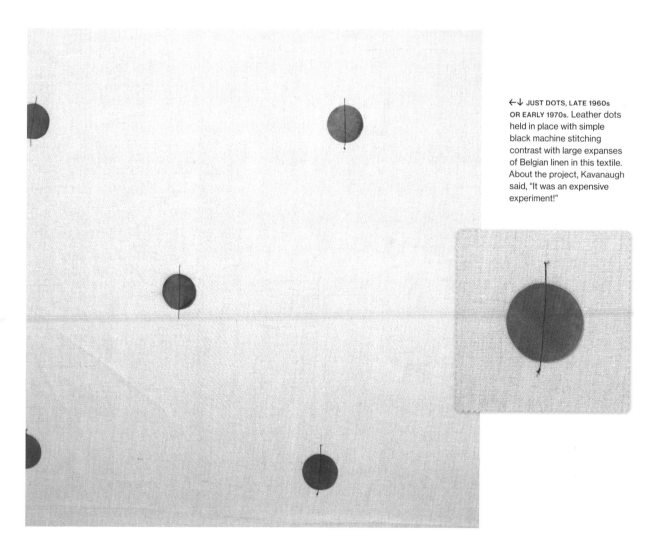

←↓ JUST DOTS, LATE 1960s OR EARLY 1970s. Leather dots held in place with simple black machine stitching contrast with large expanses of Belgian linen in this textile. About the project, Kavanaugh said, "It was an expensive experiment!"

↑ UNICORN, CA. 1950S
OR '60S. This jaunty
print on silk was also
available in blue.

→ CRYSTALS, LATE
1950S–EARLY 1960S.
This pattern, which
was printed on cotton
poplin and linen, was
inspired by Feathers,
a similar design by
Alexander Girard
produced by Herman
Miller in 1957.

→ SCATTERED BEADS,
CA. 1957.

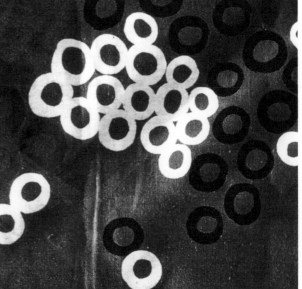

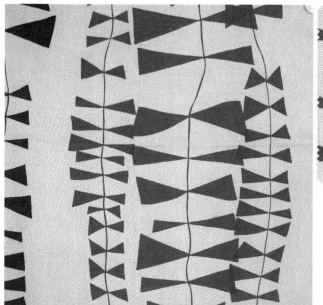

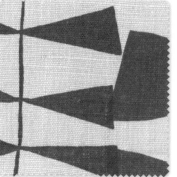

↑ Kavanaugh with
architect Bill Lou at an
exhibition of her first
textile collection for
Isabel Scott Fabrics
in 1957.

Isabel Scott Fabrics

New York-based Isabel Scott Fabrics was a small company specializing in handwoven textiles established
by weaver Isabel Scott. In the 1950s it was acquired
by Mary and Lou Roberts, who successfully expanded the
line to include commercially produced printed textiles and saw Isabel Scott Fabrics featured in five of
the Museum of Modern Art's *Good Design* exhibitions.
As luck would have it, Kavanaugh met Lou Roberts in
Detroit shortly after graduating from Cranbrook in
1952, and in just a few years the Robertses commissioned work from the young talent. Kavanaugh's first
designs featured stylized flowers, kite tails, and
beads, and were noted as "ideal for dramatizing large
windows." These prints were presented in an exhibition
in Detroit in 1957, announcing a successful relationship that would last until Lou and Mary Roberts
retired in 1974. ⁋ Kavanaugh initially designed prints
for textiles and then expanded to invitations, post-
ers, and even the company's logomark. The partnership
culminated in a journey to South Korea to research and
design a line of beautiful ikat silks.

←↑ FIELD FLOWERS,
CA. 1970. Hand-printed
on imported Swiss
batiste.

↓→ THE SEASONS,
CA. 1970. Two
colorways printed on
cotton and linen.

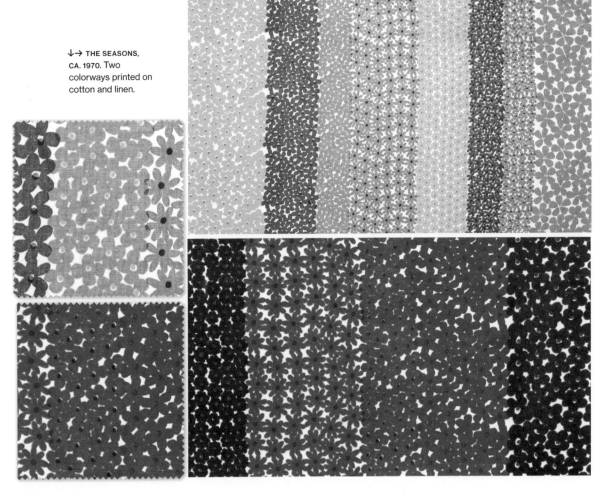

← A 1973 holiday poster was made using a split fountain screenprinting process and features calligraphy by Maury Nemoy.

← A jubilant split fountain holiday poster from 1970 with type set by Vernon Simpson Typographers.

↓ Stationery Kavanaugh designed for Isabel Scott Fabrics.

Isabel Scott Fabrics, Graphic Design Projects, 1960s–70s

↑ Kavanaugh stands by
a display of her designs.
Traditionally ikat fabrics are
made by resist dyeing silk
threads. Once the dyeing
process is complete, the
threads are carefully aligned
and woven. Because it is so
difficult to perfectly align the
threads, the final effect is a
beautiful, soft gradation at the
edges of the pattern.

Koryo Silk for Isabel Scott Fabrics, mid-1960s

Commissioned by Isabel Scott Fabrics, Kavanaugh traveled to South Korea to design and produce a line of
ikat silk fabrics. Her research in Korea included tours
of museums and private collections, to which she was
taken by Princess Julia Lee of Korea—an American who
was married to the prince of Korea. The traditional
ceramics, art, and architecture, as well as the natural landscape and encounters in daily life, became
the inspiration for her patterns. ¶ In order to produce fabrics suitable for the Western market Kavanaugh
helped develop a process of weaving fifty-two-inch
rolls, something that had never been done before. The
line included nine ikat patterns in fifty supporting
colors. Kavanaugh was recognized for her work on this
project with an award from the American Institute of
Interior Designers in 1969.

← ROSE IN KOREA, 1967. This soft floral pattern was inspired by a street vendor Kavanaugh saw walking with his bouquet of paper flowers in downtown Seoul.

← In this photo taken in 1967 in South Korea, Kavanaugh is flanked by (from left to right) Jeff Coolidge, who owned the factory that produced Isabel Scott Fabrics; an American friend of his; and Mr. Kim, who ran the factory.

↑ Kavanaugh with Mr. Kim's children (from left to right), He Jung, Jin I, and He Won.

← Factory employees outside the Koryo silk factory, near South Korea's Demilitarized Zone, in 1967.

↑ CHEVRON, 1967.
← DIAMONDS, 1967.
← MAEBONG, 1967.

→ ROSE IN KOREA, 1967.
A few of the many
color combinations
that were produced.

→ A clipping from
the *Buffalo Evening
News* featuring three
modern outfits using
ikat textiles designed
by Kavanaugh. The
clothing, which never
went into production,
was designed by
Shirley Calderon for
Tres Vites, a New York
fashion enterprise.

BUFFALO EVENING NEWS

THREE outfits from Mrs. Franz T. Stone's Tres Vite fashion collection being presented this week.

Collection Features Korean Silks

←↑ Kavanaugh posing
cheerfully in front of her
designs and (top to bottom)
a tea towel, pot holder, and
laundry bag.

→ A printed laundry bag.

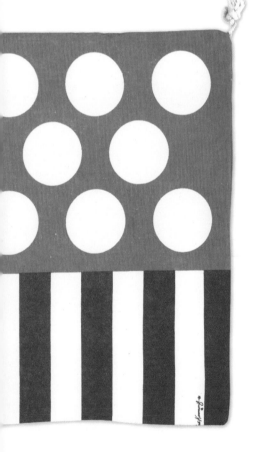

**Geré Kavanaugh houseware line prototypes,
mid-1960s**

Imagining a product line of her own, Kavanaugh
designed and created printed kitchen products
with a pop aesthetic. The cheerful speculative array included aprons, tea towels, pot
holders, and laundry bags. It was an optimistic proposal, produced in the hope that the
line would be carried by an established retail
operation, but sadly it failed to find a home.

COLOR & PATTERN BY THE YARD

BY VIRGINIA GRAY

G eré Kavanaugh wants to put color back into our lives! And she is achieving this with her bright new collection of fabrics ... 12 designs in all ... and these are but a sampling of their 38 colorways.

For more than three years she has been working on the patterns and choosing precisely the right grade of cotton to print them on. In fact, it was necessary to go all the way to Georgia to find the fine, heavier-weight cotton she had been seeking. A versatile designer, Geré had long wanted to create textiles, and now her dream is a reality with her new Geraldine Fabrics.

The patterns are whimsical, witty and folksy. Their vivid palette was greatly influenced by Geré's own attitude toward color and by upbeat folk art from all over the world. "Color keeps people happy and alive," she says. "Here in Southern California we are virtually surrounded by color—bright blue sky, flowers growing the year 'round and lots of sunshine to create it all. I have been a lover of color since I was a child back in Memphis, mixing my own paints. In fact, color has always been my signature."

Sold by the yard, these perky fabrics are intended to be made into napkins, tablecloths, draperies, bedspreads, wallhangings and even clothing. For an extra dimension, many of the motifs lend themselves to quilting. All Geraldine Fabrics are at the Pottery Barn.

Geré Kavanaugh and her dog Meeghan are pictured at left along with 11 of her 12 new fabric designs in many of the 38 total colorways available. Not pictured in the photographs is the 12th pattern, a whimsical butterfly motif called "Super Bee." Above are two of the designs shown on fabric bolts.

1. Toy Town
2. Mini Triangle
3. Dickey Birds
4. Giant Basket
5. Hail to Bea Lily
6. A Salute to Orange Julius
7. Country Flowers
8. Zoo Who
9. Tulips and Hyacinths
10. Petit Fleur
11. Puffed Dot

JAY AHREND PHOTOGRAPHS

Excerpt from article by Virginia Gray, "Color & Pattern by the Yard," LA Times Home magazine, April 24, 1977.

→ A Pottery Barn in-store summer lounging display.

← An invitation (featuring Kavanaugh's beloved dog Meeghan) for the launch of Geraldine Fabrics at Newspace, Melrose Avenue, Los Angeles, 1977.

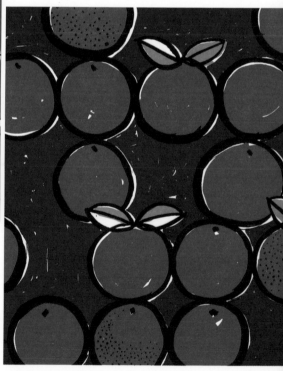

↑ DICKEY BIRDS, 1976.

→ ORANGES, 1976. This vibrant pattern of Californian oranges on cotton poplin was sold by the yard at Pottery Barn.

Geraldine Fabrics, mid-1970s

In 1975 Kavanaugh started her own line of textiles, Geraldine Fabrics. Her bold designs for
cotton poplin came in a variety of prints and
colors. She sold the fabric through Pottery Barn
as well as John Simmons, a specialty store in San
Francisco. But the market stars failed to align;
"I lost my shirt and underwear with this adven-
ture," lamented Kavanaugh.

↑ PETIT FLEUR, 1976. A dress
designed by Kavanaugh using
one of her patterns.

↑ MINI TRIANGLE, 1975.
Printed in Los Angeles
on a cotton poplin.

← SUPER BEE, CA. 1975.
A bold textile sewn
into a caftan also of
Kavanaugh's design.

↓ PUFFED DOT, 1976.

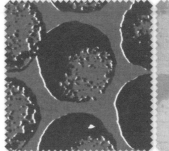

↑ As Kavanaugh recounted
to *Home Furnishings Daily* in
1964, her gold-leaf wallpaper
was based on the mosaic
she had designed for the
Ladies' Lounge at Wieboldt's
department store.

**Wallpapers for Bill Keliehor,
Kyoto, Japan, mid-1960s**

Wallpaper designs by Kavanaugh were printed by Bill
Keliehor with stencils he created in his Kyoto-
based enterprise. The design was printed onto *washi*—
traditional Japanese paper made by hand from local
tree or bush fibers—and then metal leaf was applied.

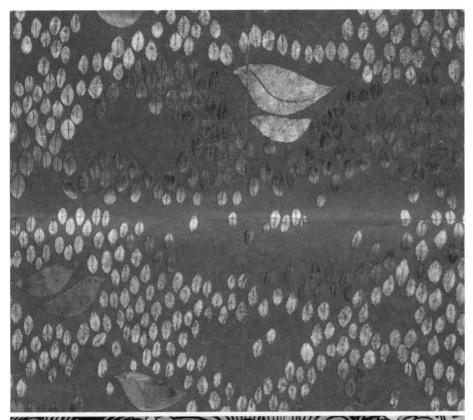

← ALL A TWITTER, CA. 1966.
This design was printed
on heavy paper stock the
width of a shoji screen.

← SPICE FLOWER, CA. 1967.
Ming yea paper, gold
leaf, and silkscreen. The
silver colorway of this
wallpaper was used in the
salon at Joseph Magnin's
Mountain View store (see
page 66).

← GIANT FLOWERS,
CA. 1970. Kavanaugh
designed this playful
print using cut paper.

→ DAISY CHAIN, CA. 1962.
This design was included
in the 1962 exhibition
California Design Eight
and published in the
accompanying catalog.

**Wallpapers for Bob Mitchell Designs,
California, 1960–70s**

← SCATTERED BEADS,
CA. 1970. This design
may have been inspired
by a print of the same
name that Kavanaugh
had created for Isabel
Scott Fabrics in the
1950s.

I ntroducing
the brightest,
smartest
new ways to
wrap up
your holiday
gifting...
Six imaginative
gift wrap
patterns in
a sparkling array
of colors —
created by a
leading designer
and especially
selected by
House Beautiful —
all you need
for Christmas or
Hanukkah or
for any festive
occasion to
dress presents
that are truly...

too pretty to open!

Smart, stylish, incredibly versatile, the collection is marked by subtleties of color and by preciseness of pattern

For CPS Industries Inc., Kavanaugh designed six patterns for metallic gift papers inspired by concepts the publication identifies as "Shibui," "The Mix," "The New Romanticism," and "Country Chic." Papers identified by number are 1: "Oriental"; 2: "Zig Zag"; 3: "Plum Blossom."

Excerpt from *House Beautiful*, date unknown.

interiors

In 1958 Kavanaugh completed one of her first residential commissions: designing the interiors of the Birmingham, Michigan, home of a local engineer, V. C. Wagner. After leaving Gruen Associates in 1964, Kavanaugh continued to work with Gruen client Toys by Roy, designing everything from the store's interior to its graphics. That same year, Kavanaugh was also hired to design the restaurant for a J. L. Hudson Company department store in the Gruen-designed Westland Shopping Center in a suburb of Detroit. Diners ascended to the second-floor restaurant via an open stairway with landings dotted with wire sculptures by artist Ruth Asawa, which were commissioned by Kavanaugh. ¶ By 1970 Gere Kavanaugh/Designs was a thriving concern with a handful of employees juggling a steady stream of projects, many of which came through referrals. And, significantly, her work began appearing in both popular magazines and trade publications. At a party in the late 1960s, Kavanaugh had met Adrienne Hall, a founder of Hall & Levine, the first advertising agency in America led by women. From this serendipitous encounter Kavanaugh was hired to design the firm's office, which was in one of Los Angeles's first high-rise towers. Kavanaugh's approach was fresh—Californian and feminine without the frill. The outcome was so warmly embraced by the client that Hall asked Kavanaugh to design her home—a pad so strikingly balanced for both entertaining and family that it was featured in *House Beautiful*. Another project, published in *Cosmopolitan* magazine, was a bright, cheap-and-cheerful apartment decorated for the single Cosmo Girl to play out her entertaining fantasies. ¶ Whether a simple but warm office interior, a bohemian bachelorette apartment, or a gallery for prized treasures, Kavanaugh's designs were characterized by acute attention to the ineffable details that make an environment distinct. All were works of wonder and delight.

→ Bob Snyder, an architect and head of Cranbrook's architecture studio, hired Kavanaugh to design the interiors of the house he designed. Kavanaugh designed several pieces of furniture, including tables, bookcase storage wall, and cherry wood harvest table, as well as the daisy photo mural hanging on the living room wall. The house was featured in a 1964 issue of *Home Furnishings Daily*.

V. C. Wagner House,
Birmingham, Michigan, 1958

Toys by Roy, Albuquerque, 1961–74

This toy-store interior was initiated while Kavanaugh was head of interiors at Victor Gruen Associates. Her colorful scheme of geometric patterns resembling wooden building blocks serves as a unifying motif for lighting, display fixtures, and graphic elements, creating an imaginary village of play. Her relationship with Toys by Roy would continue well past her tenure at Gruen.

↑ Kavanaugh created this print using rubber stamps she had made from tire inner tubes. The commercially printed wrapping paper was available in a number of color combinations.

→→ Toys by Roy interior.

→ A gift tag bearing the rocking horse logo Kavanaugh designed for Toys by Roy.

J. L. Hudson Terrace Restaurant and Cafeteria, Westland Shopping Center, Detroit, 1965

Treelike sculptures by artist Ruth Asawa lined the stairs leading up to this restaurant and cafeteria, located on the second floor of the Westland Shopping Center, suggesting a garden path. On the terrace a full-service restaurant overlooked the mall plaza. Yellow banners were suspended overhead, creating the impression of a striped awning, while speckled carpeting was like a field of flowers. In the cafeteria ceramic birds fabricated by Los Angeles artist Dora De Larios were mounted on walls adorned with a whimsical wallpaper of black trees on a white ground, a pattern designed by Kavanaugh and, as she recalls, printed by Bob Mitchell Designs. Uniting the rooms were red-and-white candy-striped light fixtures produced by Venini, the renowned Murano glass manufacturer.

↓ A treelike wire sculpture by Ruth Asawa, detail.

↓↓ A swatch of speckled carpet that resembled a field of flowers.

↓→ The restaurant seen from the plaza below. The stairway features Ruth Asawa sculptures that were commissioned by Kavanaugh as part of the restaurant design project.

→→ Cafeteria.

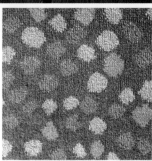

←↑ In the reception area typographic serigraphs by Sister Corita Kent adorned the walls — their phrases picked for their appropriateness to the advertising world. White telephones, typewriters, and adding machines completed the open, optimistic feel. Doors were finished in apricot-colored lacquer.

↓ The office of one of the partners. Kavanaugh placed greenery throughout the space, earning the Hall & Levine office the nickname "greenhouse in the sky."

↓→ The conference room – bright, airy, and fresh – featured gleaming white tiled floors. According to legend, this detail so enchanted clients from Catalina, the swimwear company, that they immediately engaged the agency. Custom furniture designed by Kavanaugh was paired with lemon-yellow and candy-cream-orange textiles by Isabel Scott Fabrics.

Hall & Levine, Century City, Los Angeles, 1970

Owned and operated by women, Hall & Levine advertising agency handled "big boy" accounts whose products targeted female consumers, including Catalina Swimwear, Max Factor, and Neutrogena. Wishing to deviate from the typically formal, masculine look of Madison Avenue offices, partners Adrienne Hall and Joan Levine asked Kavanaugh to design a space that exuded a Southern California vibe, where both genders would feel at home.

The Leonard and Judith Gertler Home, Santa Monica, 1970

For this treehouse-like residential extension by Ray Kappe, an architect inspired by the post-and-beam California Case Study Houses, Kavanaugh chose an aesthetic that embraced contemporary craft. The Gertler house featured the Chopping Block on Wheels bar cart complete with bicycle tires, created by fellow California designer Bill W. Sanders in 1964. Some of the other pieces in this photograph were placed as props, including a vase and pillows from Kavanaugh's own collection.

the new romanticism

By JAMES De LONG ☐ True romanticism is an expression of now. It emphasizes individualism and original thought. It does not live in the past but draws freely on the spirit of the past to refresh its own spontaneous creativity. This contemporary house of Mr. and Mrs. Maurice Arthur Hall is an excellent example of romanticism in action. Inspired by travels in Mexico and their collection of primitive and pre-Columbian art, the Halls asked Architect Perry Neuschatz, his associate, Gary Call, and Interior Designer Geré Kavanaugh to distill the essence of California's Spanish past in the design of their Beverly Hills home. This thoughtful backward glance has tempered their architecture with the softening edges of an older culture, but it still is very much a house of today.

MAX ECKERT

IN CALIFORNIA THE GRACIOUS HACIENDA
IN CONTEMPORARY DRESS

HALL HOUSE, BEVERLY HILLS, 1972. Described as a "gracious hacienda in contemporary dress," Hall & Levine partner Adrienne Hall's private residence shows what Kavanaugh could do when given free rein. The space was designed to accommodate four active children, regular fundraising soirées and other social events, and the couple's noted pre-Columbian and folk art collections.

Furnish All at Once!

You've moved into a beautiful new apartment. Your *budget* says you ought to decorate gradually…but you want to do it *now*. Meet Melissa, who furnished three sensational rooms (and *didn't* go broke) in just two weeks! Give you any ideas?

Melissa's expensive-looking dining table *(right)* is simply two painted doors placed side by side on square blocks, which can also be stacked to form coffee table *(bottom, left)*. Long, lean sofa *(bottom, right)* is made from two more doors placed end to end on blocks, layered with foam rubber, then covered with fabric and topped with pillows. Missy's handsome and willing neighbor helped her paint wall to save painter's fee. With a little inventiveness, a girl can save *lots* of money!

Since Melissa's rooms look out on sunny patio *(see floor plan)*, she decorates with plants *(right)*— nurtured cuttings free from the garden—to emphasize view. Her apartment in Tustin, California, is in "The Californian" community development *(above)* by Leadership Housing, Inc. Architect: Backen, Arrigoni & Ross.

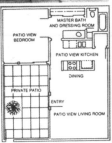

MASTER BATH AND DRESSING ROOM
PATIO VIEW BEDROOM
PATIO VIEW KITCHEN
DINING
PRIVATE PATIO
ENTRY
PATIO VIEW LIVING ROOM

DECORATING EDITOR: KAREN FISHER
Text: Robin Wagner
Photos: Elyse Lewin; Interior Design: Gere Kavanaugh

COSMO HOUSE, CA. 1972. Kavanaugh was hired by a Chicago PR firm to create this cheerful, affordable living space for the liberated gal whose lifestyle bible was *Cosmopolitan* magazine. The challenge was to create a space that would be colorful, conducive to entertaining, and look terrific in a magazine layout. A cardboard rocker by Frank Gehry is featured at lower left.

Excerpt from *Cosmopolitan* magazine 1972.

Kavanaugh's model is full of charming details such as a potted palm tree, a Matisse print, and a nesting bird decoration between the twin beds. Electric-orange doors open onto hallways with supergraphics of pineapples and flowers.

Model for Developer Gerald D. Hines, 1975

A referral from *House Beautiful* editor Wally Guenther landed Kavanaugh the commission to design the interiors of a resort for real estate developer Gerald D. Hines, who had just completed Pennzoil Place in Houston, Texas, with architects Philip Johnson and John Burgee. As Hines failed to secure financing, the project never made it beyond the presentation phase. According to Kavanaugh, all that remains is this dollhouse-size model, which nevertheless reflects the light and airy Floridian feel the client sought.

Einstein House, Los Angeles, 1989

For art collectors Cliff and Mandy Einstein, Kavanaugh
created a gallery-like living space to display the
couple's copious and diverse art holdings. Her striking design, focused on simplicity and craftsmanship,
was featured in several magazines across the globe.

←↓ Kavanaugh's
comprehensive vision
often exceeded the
limits of interiors.
On this design
by architect Ron
Goldman, Kavanaugh
draws proposed
colored treatments.

← This sitting room includes a 1983 Park coffee table by Ettore Sottsass and a 1982 Lido sofa by Michele De Lucchi. The small table tucked between black armchairs, at right, was designed by Kavanaugh. Artworks include a Magdalena Abakanowicz sculpture.

↑ The club room features a sunken seating area. At the center is a coffee table surrounded by a Memphis-style tile arrangement by Los Angeles artist Marlo Bartels. Above the fireplace hangs a painting by Tony Berlant. Against the far wall, under a painting by Ed Moses, are four Cesca chairs by Marcel Breuer.

↑ Artifacts line the sixty-thousand-square-foot offices of Neutrogena. Kavanaugh amusedly recalls arguments among the staff over who would get to display their favorite piece in their office.

Neutrogena Corporate Offices, Los Angeles, 1994

A thirty-year relationship with Neutrogena CEO and president Lloyd Cotsen led to Kavanaugh being hired to design the interiors for their corporate headquarters. The two floors of office space, occupying separate rectangular buildings connected by a glass pyramid-capped atrium designed by Ellerbe Becket, were home to an extensive collection of ethnographic and folk art. Built over many years by Cotsen, the diverse and enviable accumulation in a vast range of media included Native American textiles, Mexican pottery, and, in particular, Japanese baskets, alongside an assortment of other objects from cultures around the world. Kavanaugh painted the walls with bold blocks of color in multitudes of shades and hues to offset the varied artifacts. The colors had been "collected" over many years by Kavanaugh and were inspired by all aspects of her life.

To bathe the corridors in color, Kavanaugh developed a range of eggshell-finish paints, which were applied to the walls with giant squeegees so no brush marks would show.

→ Handwoven textiles hang on a dynamic blue wall.

→ Striking bubblegum-pink shelves are home to the unique, multifarious ornaments and sculptures.

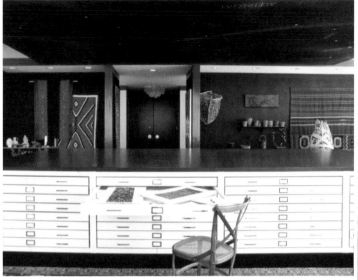

In the study area, objects from Cotsen's collection surround a central bank of flat files containing artifacts from many cultures. Mirroring the expansive midnight blue surface is a ceiling feature, adorned with the celestial map of Cotsen's birthday.

↑ A wooden relic from a seventeenth-century Portuguese ship glances toward the study area and library.

Private Gallery for Lloyd Cotsen, Los Angeles, 2003

Following the Neutrogena headquarters project, Cotsen asked Kavanaugh to convert a three-bedroom condominium into a private gallery where he could enjoy his vast collection and make it available to researchers. To create the space, Kavanaugh donned an architectural cap, stripping the unit down to its studs and enclosing the balcony. She created two long rooms: one, with the kitchen, bathroom, and areas for lounging and sleeping, was intimate and domestic; the other, boasting a bank of windows overlooking the Los Angeles skyline, was devoted to the collection.

" I could write about Gere as the indomitable lady with the chicken purse and the forthright voice, the I'd-like-to-be-like-that-when-I'm-old lady, the undersung, multifaceted designer who retains enough wide-eyed wonder to see the marvels around us in the everyday. Others will probably fill that slot – there is no dearth of admirers. But I'm going to write about Gere's impact on me before I even knew she existed. ❀ Looking through images for this book earlier this year, I was stunned by a moment of recognition of two photos of my father's house as it was when he bought it from a very design-forward couple, who I believe had hired Gere. I wish more photos of that exuberant iteration of the house remained – bright, deep colors defining each room; the overstuffed sage-green sofa matching the living room walls; the bougainvillea-pink kitchen; the dramatic, massive, glossy burl-wood dining table; the cheap plastic cubes turned designer pedestals by a coat of matching paint. I loved that house from the minute I saw it as a teenager in the late 1980s – the whimsical, bold moves that elevated a lovely (if standard) 1930s Hollywood house into a place that was exciting and stylish and cozy all at the same time. Those brilliant colors were my introduction to Gere, though I didn't know it at the time. They were my firsthand experience of the impact of color and detail and scale in everyday life, and undoubtedly influenced my development as a designer. ❋

 Eventually, in 2002, my dad's friend Frank [Gehry] helped remodel the house (with the help of a young associate from his office, Rachel Allen), updating the kitchen, making a home office, reducing some architectural details. This was a new kind of lovely, all painted a crisp architect's white, erasing the '80s altogether. Except for the guest bedroom where I stayed. The resonant goldenrod pigment on the walls, glowing beyond reason at the end of the day, the quality of paint synchronized with the quality of light, the bright blue trim going beyond the possibilities of sky — all combined to make a feeling, a sense of place, a sense of time that still transports me when I think back to it. I made sure that they didn't touch that alchemical paint. They all teased me about being attached to the color, but now I realize it was a connection to Gere, to Gere's perfect work. ❞ — Jessica Fleischmann, Founder and Creative Director, Still Room (and daughter of Ernest Fleischmann, former Executive Director, Los Angeles Philharmonic)

furniture

Kavanaugh first tried her hand at furniture design as a student at Cranbrook. Cross-disciplinary experimentation was part of the school's ethos, and furniture design in particular was in the school's blood. From her first attempt at designing a multipurpose table, Kavanaugh's furniture was as much about fantasy as it was function. Some works didn't make it beyond fanciful drawings or prototypes, while others were produced for client projects. Occasionally a piece made it to the manufacturing stage, including the Market Umbrella—originally designed in 1968 for Soupçon restaurant in the South Coast Plaza Joseph Magnin store—and Gere's Chair in the 1970s. Several of Kavanaugh's furniture designs were featured in the Pasadena Art Museum's *California Design* exhibitions and published in the corresponding exhibition catalogs. ¶ Kavanaugh created one cluster of projects in the 1970s with Sonotubes—cardboard tubes normally used to shape concrete pillars in construction projects. Although cardboard construction was a trend—Frank Gehry, Works West, and Marget Larsen and Robert Brewster Freeman of Intrinsics all created furniture from the material—Kavanaugh was most likely inspired to use Sonotubes after encountering Los Angeles-based artists also working with the material. ¶ Some of Kavanaugh's furniture concepts were driven by historical or cultural influences, such as Pennsylvania Dutch and Shaker furnishings and Japanese torii structures. Nature was another wealth of inspiration, as seen in a series of whimsical steel table pedestals resembling insects, flora, and fauna. For whatever furniture she created, fun was her most frequent muse.

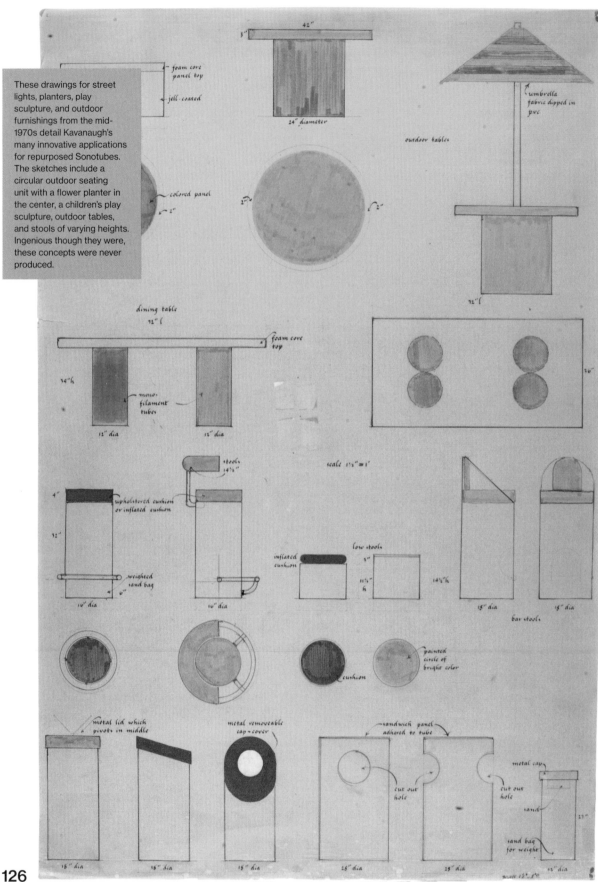

These drawings for street lights, planters, play sculpture, and outdoor furnishings from the mid-1970s detail Kavanaugh's many innovative applications for repurposed Sonotubes. The sketches include a circular outdoor seating unit with a flower planter in the center, a children's play sculpture, outdoor tables, and stools of varying heights. Ingenious though they were, these concepts were never produced.

42"

foam core panel top

jell-coated

24" diameter

umbrella fabric dipped in pvc

outdoor table

colored panel

1"

2"

2"

72" l

dining table
72" l

foam core top

34"h

mono-filament tubes

12" dia

15" dia

36"

scale 1½" = 1'

stool
14½"

upholstered cushion or inflated cushion

4"

32"

low stool

inflated cushion

1"

weighted sand bag

9"

11½" h

14½" h

16" dia

16" dia

15" dia

15" dia

bar stool

painted circle of bright color

cushion

metal lid which pivots in middle

metal removeable cap - cover

sandwich panel adhered to tube

metal cap

cut out hole

cut out hole

sand

27"

sand bag for weight

18" dia

18" dia

18" dia

18" dia

18" dia

scale 1½"-1'0"

18" dia

126

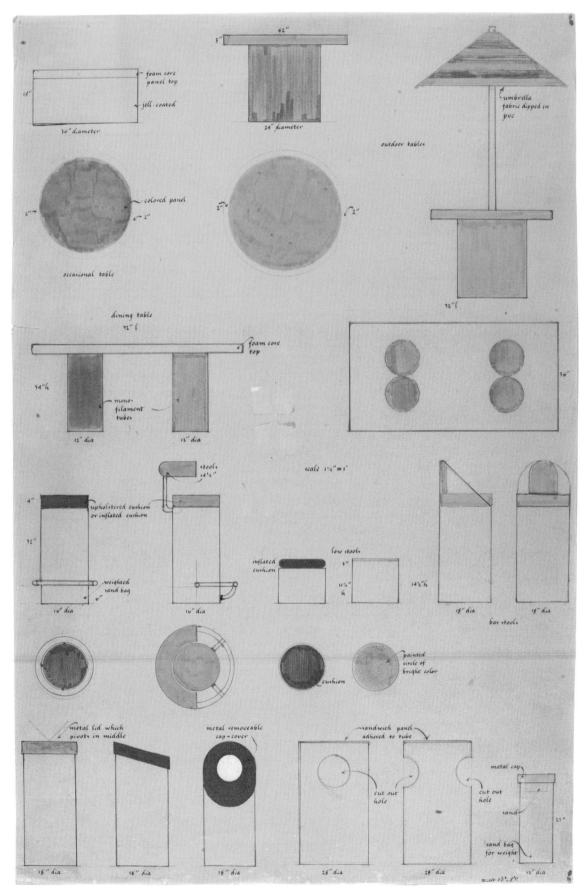

foam core panel top

jell-coated

15"

30" diameter

42"

3"

24 diameter

outdoor tables

umbrella fabric dipped in pvc

colored panel

occasional table

2"

2"

2"

2"

72"l

dining table
72"l

foam core top

34"h

mono-filament tubes

12" dia

12" dia

36"

scale 1½"=1'

stools
14½"

upholstered cushion or inflated cushion

4"

32"

inflated cushion

low stools

1"

11½" h

14½"h

weighted sand bag

6"

10" dia

10" dia

15" dia

15" dia

bar stools

cushion

painted circle of bright color

metal lid which pivots in middle

metal removeable cap - cover

sandwich panel adhered to tube

metal cap

cut out hole

cut out hole

sand

23"

sand bag for weight

18" dia

18" dia

18" dia

25" dia

25" dia

12" dia

scale 1½"=1'0

127

↑→ **GERE'S CHAIR**, 1980s. Produced by Images of America and sold in showrooms across the country, this design was inspired by torii structures found in Japanese temples. Kavanaugh used the chair for seating when she designed the research room interior for the Richard Nixon Presidential Library and Museum in Yorba Linda, California. Gere's Chair was made of a high-grade tubular steel base and a polyurethane foam–coated molded plywood seat that could be covered with fabric or leather upholstery. Kavanaugh's supersized gouache illustration, above, shows the chair in various views.

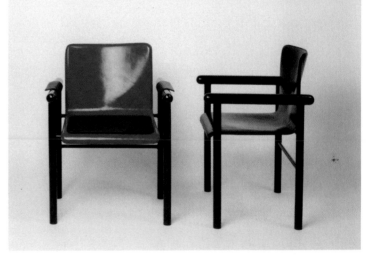

↑ **SHAKER SETTEE, EARLY 1960s.**
Kavanaugh's gouache design drawing
for a settee that was inspired by
the simplicity and timelessness of
early American furniture, particularly
work by the Pennsylvania Dutch
and Shakers. It was produced by
craftsman David Edberg and featured
in the Pasadena Art Museum's 1965
exhibition *California Design Nine*. It now
resides in Kavanaugh's living room, seen
on page 193.

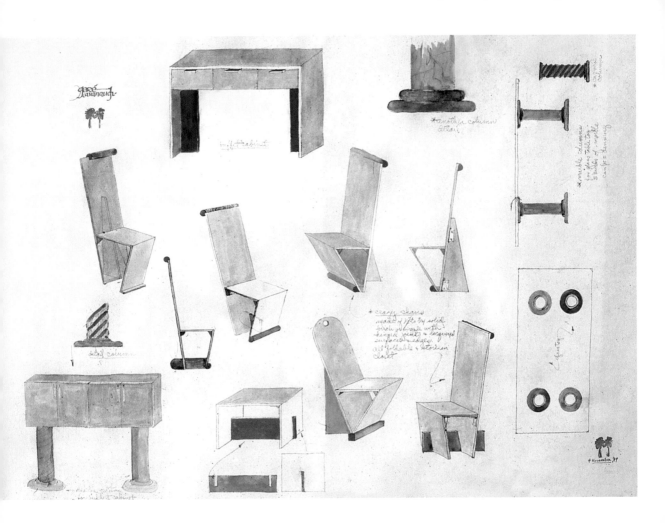

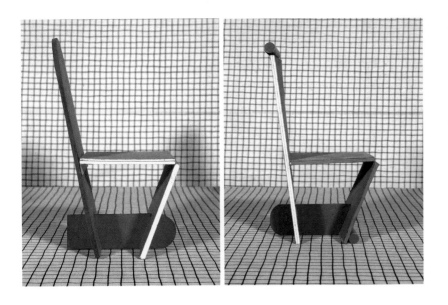

↑ CRAZY CHAIR, 1979–85. This colorful 1979 sketch details a series of postmodern furnishings. The designs were influenced by Rudolph Schindler's plywood chairs, which Kavanaugh had experienced firsthand in her Schindler-designed doctor's office.

← Two petite Crazy Chair models. In 1985 Kavanaugh had several of the chairs fabricated for her office, but she never sought wider production. Documentation of the realized chairs can be seen in Kavanaugh's Angelino Heights living room, seen on page 193.

←↓ **BUNGALOW CHAIR, LATE 1970s.** Kavanaugh wrote of the chair, "A Romantic Chair or The Bungalow Chair to be made of mahogany and stained or lacquered deep green or deep maroon red, a GK fabric or jacquard weave." In the drawing below she shows options for color, cushions, and fabrics.

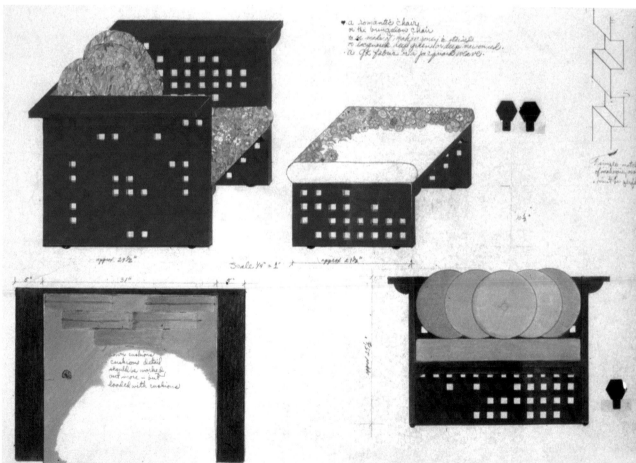

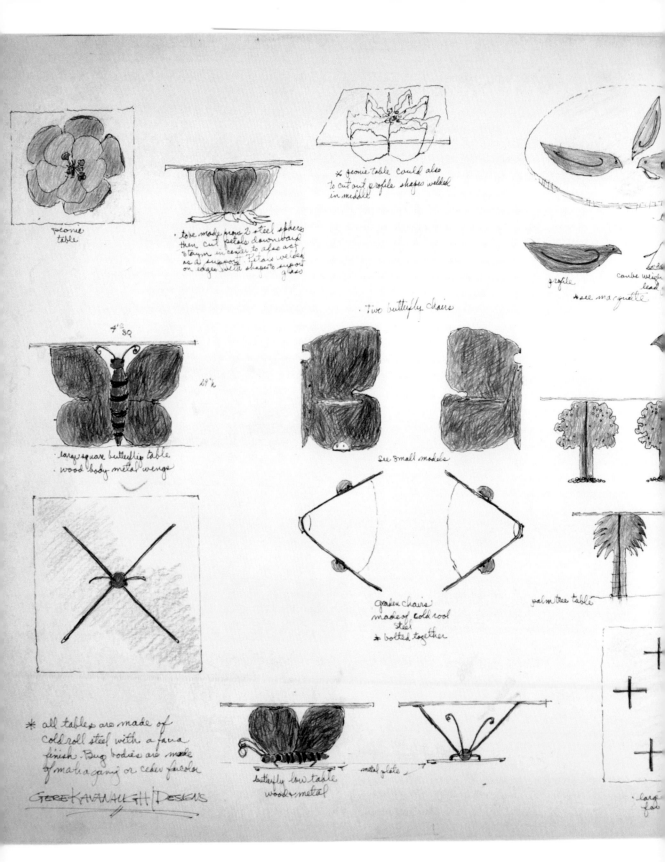

peonie
table

* peonie table could also
be cut out profile shapes welded
in middle

• table made from 2 steel spheres
then cut petals downward
staying in center to also act
as a support. Petals welded
on edges with shapes to support
glass

profile

* see maquette

can be weight
lead

• Two butterfly chairs

4'½
SQ

29"½

• large square butterfly table
• wood body metal wings

see small models

garden chairs
made of cold roll
steel
* bolted together

palm tree table

* all tables are made of
cold roll steel with a faux
finish. Bug bodies are made
of mahogany or cedar faux color

GERE KAVANAUGH DESIGNS

butterfly low table
wood + metal

metal plate

• large
fau

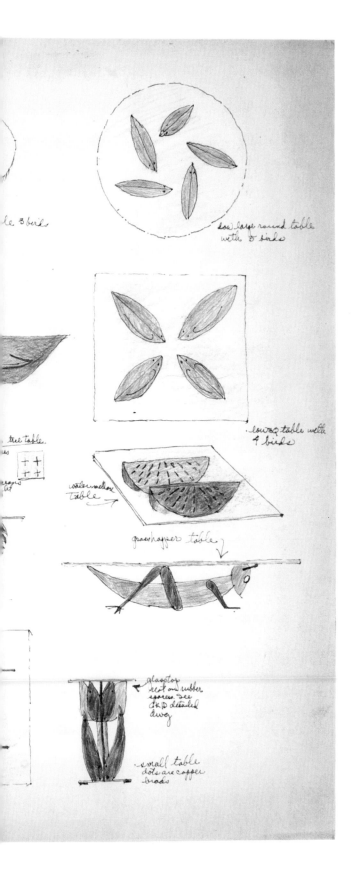

↑ The butterfly chair, fabricated from cold-rolled steel by architect and metal fabricator Tom Farrage in the early 2000s.

← These sketches for glass-topped tables with oversized bird, insect, watermelon, and flora bases and a butterfly garden chair were drawn in the 1990s. This series marries Kavanaugh's fascination with oversized scale and her love for the natural world.

urban
scale

→ Kavanaugh was
commissioned by architect
Louis G. Redstone, a fellow
Cranbrook graduate, to
design this floral mural for
a shopping center in Detroit.
The mural is made from
glazed bricks and was
completed in 1958.

Kavanaugh thought big, so large-scale urban projects were a perfect fit. Some of her outsized ideas
were so spirited on paper that they took on a life of
their own, despite never having been realized. Others
were built and made major statements, beginning with
a fantastical mosaic mural for a Detroit-area shopping center. ¶ Kavanaugh's 1971 Fantasy Flowers
concept for the Highland Mall in Austin, the city's
first suburban shopping center, was nothing short of a
moveable extravaganza of color and scale. Her design
was radically upbeat, with enormous, brightly colored steel flowers that could be relocated anywhere
within the mall—a moveable garden of delight! ¶ In
2002 Kavanaugh was the first interior designer to be
awarded the City of Los Angeles Individual Artist
Fellowship, a grant that honors established artists of diverse practices and funds a new project by
each recipient. She used her funding to bring to life
a childhood obsession with clustering pigeons. Her
concept was to create a grouping of larger-than-life
bird sculptures in a plaza, where they could both serve
as seating and provide a moment of urban delight to
passersby.

This presentation drawing for the Rouse Company (probably from the 1970s) showed "what could be done design-wise with shopping centers." To enthusiastically convey her concept, Kavanaugh added hand-drawn balloons, rubber-stamped cars, and cutout photographs. She never had the chance to propose the design to the client.

←↑ Highland Mall Center Court.

Highland Mall, Austin, Texas, 1971

Color, fun, fantasy, and flexibility defined Kavanaugh's approach to this project in an Austin suburb commissioned by developers the Rouse Company. Giant banners animated the lofty space, while superscale mobile flower sculptures were designed to be scattered throughout the mall, ensuring that the space would always be fresh and lively.

→→ **FANTASY FLOWERS, 1971.** Produced in Los Angeles, these supersized sculptural elements, three to eleven feet tall, appear here just after fabrication, before heading to the Highland Mall in Austin, Texas.

↑ Maquette for Fantasy Flowers, complete with scale figures.

In these 1980s concept sketches for Union Station, the transit hub of Los Angeles, Kavanaugh envisioned signs made from topiaries or red metal resembling a railroad trestle.

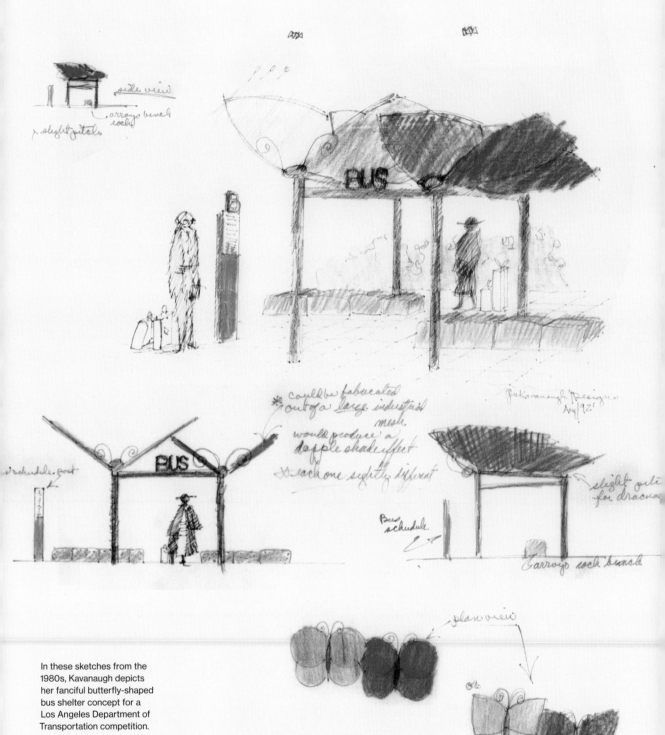

In these sketches from the 1980s, Kavanaugh depicts her fanciful butterfly-shaped bus shelter concept for a Los Angeles Department of Transportation competition.

4'0
wide

4'0
wide

✱ pear sculpture for
a plaza or park
casted iron / black
or bronze

A slice of fruit from a nearby
pear sculpture becomes a bench
in these imaginative concept
sketches from the 1980s.
Although Kavanaugh presented
the design to "everyone in
the country," it has yet to be
produced.

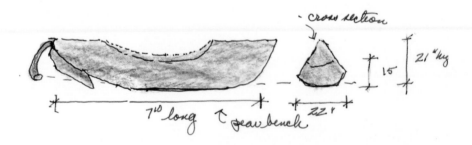

- cross section

21 "hy

15

7'0 long   ↑ pear bench   22'

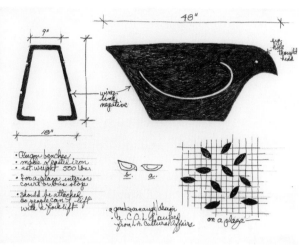

**City of Los Angeles Individual
Artist Fellowship Project, 2009**

↑ In these concept
sketches, Kavanaugh
envisions a flock
of pigeon benches
scattered around a
plaza or courtyard.

← Although Kavanaugh
was only able to realize
a single cast-iron bird,
her digital rendering
shows a flock of these
weighty creatures
gathered in Noguchi
Plaza, Little Tokyo, in
downtown Los Angeles.

exhibitions

"A prolific designer. A comprehensive designer," *Interiors* magazine said of Kavanaugh in a review of her exhibition designs in its August 1980 issue. As a designer and occasional curator, Kavanaugh has made significant cultural contributions over the course of her long career. Sadly, many of her efforts have been poorly documented and have faded from memory. *Islands in the Land: Folk Art and Objects* was one such exhibition. Held at the Pasadena Art Museum from late 1972 to early 1973, this exhibition of traditional crafts from Appalachia and New Mexico's Rio Grande Valley was organized by the museum's design curator, Eudorah Moore. (It was Moore who was also responsible for the legendary *California Design* exhibitions from 1962 to 1976.) For the exhibition design, Kavanaugh aimed to "destroy the pristine interior of the museum, setting the stage to dramatize the environment from which the objects came." ¶ Kavanaugh also designed two exhibitions of note for the ARCO Center for Visual Art in Los Angeles. For the 1977 *Fantasy Clothes, Fantastic Costumes*, which featured five Los Angeles artists, she crafted an eye-catching title wall with block letters formed from shimmering plastic disks. And for *Los Angeles and the Palm Tree: Image of a City*, a loving contribution to the Los Angeles 1984 Olympic Games, she created simple, abstracted interpretations of the city's landscape as backdrops to works of art that featured the iconic tree. ¶ But the standout moment in Kavanaugh's history with exhibitions—and possibly her whole career—was 1983's NEA-funded *Home Sweet Home: American Domestic Vernacular Architecture*, which she conceived and cocurated with famed architect Charles Moore. Produced by the Craft and Folk Art Museum in Los Angeles, *Home Sweet Home* investigated "the history of American domestic architecture, regional designs, houseboats, mobile homes, children's construction toys, and adobe, wooden, and stucco houses." The show, a series of exhibitions that spanned thirteen venues across Los Angeles, was accompanied by a symposium at the University of California, Los Angeles, and an exhibition catalog.

↑ *HOME SWEET HOME*, 1983. This exhibition catalog published by Rizzoli for the show that Kavanaugh cocurated is the only documentation that remains. She also designed the cover.

LA AND THE PALM TREE: THE IMAGE OF A CITY, LOS ANGELES, 1984. Held at the ARCO Center for Visual Art in downtown Los Angeles in celebration of the 1984 Summer Olympics, this exhibition celebrated and interrogated the city's most emblematic tree. Twenty-five thousand palm trees had been planted to beautify the city for the previous Los Angeles Olympic Games in 1932, creating thousands of jobs in the process. The exhibition featured artworks in which these iconic soldiers of the LA landscape figured.

Islands in the Land,
Pasadena Art Museum, 1972–73

Celebrated in the press as a triumph of curatorial vision
and design innovation, this exhibition of three thousand
traditional objects from Appalachia and the Rio Grande
Valley of New Mexico was organized by Eudorah Moore and
designed by Kavanaugh. Her challenge was to create a sense
of the environments from which the objects had emerged while
acknowledging and honoring their makers. She employed sky-
blue and white paint as well as cut cardboard to distinguish
the two regions. With this limited palette she managed to
channel the dry mesas and stepped adobes of the New Mexico
landscape and the rolling hills of rural Appalachia. Mural-
size photographs provided further detail about each setting.
To convey the design theme, Kavanaugh utilized humble
wooden platforms made by a local crating company.

← The outline of an adobe church supplied an appropriately dramatic backdrop for this display of crucifixes and other objects from the New Mexican Rio Grande Valley.

↓ The Appalachian section of the exhibition featured handwoven baskets, brooms, and tools, with mural-scale photographs by Richard Gross celebrating their makers.

Gere Kavanaugh:

A Prolific Designer

"**A** comprehensive designer" who will do any project "that comes along the pike," is Gere Kavanaugh's self-description. Over the past 15 years as an independent designer, she has to her credit: interiors (primarily of the commercial category, with an occasional residential commission accepted if the prospect appeals to her); graphics; textiles (both for trade sources and her own firm Geraldine Fabrics); and special exhibitions in her adopted city of Los Angeles. It is on this last category that we concentrate, for it represents an aspect of design slightly removed from our everyday contact.

Ms. Kavanaugh delved into exhibition design some eight years ago with a project, for the Pasadena Museum, entitled "Islands in the Land"; the exhibit was based on display of traditional crafts from Appalachia and the Rio Grande Valley in New Mexico. Over the years, she has developed her own approach to the metier—an approach that she terms particularly suited to southern California. She is drawn to individual objects and seeks to show them in their relevant surroundings. She is not interested in isolated objects, nor in display for display's sake. "I am concerned more with the objects and their place in a particular society than I am with creating a scholarly treatise on a subject," she says. "On the Coast, exhibits are not as 'pure' as they are in the East. Here, they are more human."

Opposite, we show three of the numerous exhibitions to her credit. "Fantasy Clothes, Fantastic Costumes" was held three years ago at the Arco Visual Center. "The Greek Ethos" was at the Craft and Folk Art Museum; "Robert O. Anderson's Indian Collection" was at the Arco Visual Center.

The interior project, a Hallmark store in Arco Plaza, Los Angeles, shows how a designer can also work as a merchandiser. The key design elements created for this all-white shell are a series of paper decorations based on seasonal motifs. They are hung from the ceiling and changed, of course, periodically. Recognizing the sales potential of these items, the Hallmark Corporation made them part of the merchandise offering and now they account for more than $1 million in yearly sales, according to the designer. Further, they have been integrated into the entire Hallmark chain of stores —"from Honolulu to Cape Cod," she says.

Gere Kavanaugh, a native of Memphis, attended art school from the age of eight, starting at the Memphis Academy of Arts. She continued at that institution and earned a B.F.A. degree, and then an M.F.A. degree from Cranbrook Academy of Arts. She worked as a designer for General Motors and then moved to the West Coast to work for Victor Gruen. Currently, she is involved in designing a restaurant for the May Company and branch interiors for the Wells Fargo Bank. Recently she also received funding from the National Endowment for the Arts to mount an exhibition called "Indigenous Architecture of the U.S.A." for the Los Angeles Crafts and Folk Art Museum in 1982. Charles Moore is to be co-curator. **E.C.**

Five women contributed their interpretation of clothing/costumes as conceptual art for the exhibition Fantasy Clothes, Fantastic Costumes." Ms. Kavanaugh painted the background a purple/black/brown shade and created the sign of shimmering plastic discs.

"The Greek Ethos" show came about when a guest curator, Basil Genkins, wanted to display ethnic artifacts owned by residents of L.A.'s Greek community. Ms. Kavanaugh's task was "to create an atmosphere or environment that told something about the objects," she says.

Some 500 artifacts from the private collection of Arco board chairman Robert O. Anderson were displayed at the Arco Visual Center. Objects included blankets, bags and a medicine doll.

anaugh became involved in merchandising for the Hall-
rporation when her seasonal design elements became
ed into the card collection for subsequent sales. Ac-
to the designer, these elements account for almost
n in yearly sales.

Excerpt from *Interior Design* magazine, August 1980

toys & products

Kavanaugh's love of craft and objects surfaced in her designs throughout her career. In the 1950s and '60s, she created handmade wooden crèches and other products as affectionate tributes to her favorite holiday—Christmas! Originally displayed in her home, they reappeared in 2006 alongside newer designs when Bridget Burke hired Kavanaugh to design holiday products that would offer a fresher perspective to the more traditional Christmas collectibles produced by the giftware wholesaler Department 56. But due to turmoil at the Minnesota-based company, Kavanaugh's work never went into production. When Burke went on to join Target, Kavanaugh proposed to her a line of charming butterfly and bug ornaments. Delightful though they were, this concept never left the ground, either. ¶ Other projects Kavanaugh generated were more speculative. In 1966, to accompany an article in *Progressive Architecture* magazine about modern toys that encouraged a sense of "form, relationship, and integrity" in children, she designed a wooden city block set. In a somewhat altered version, this city-planning toy prototype, which resides in the collection of the Los Angeles County Museum of Art, was finally put into production in 2015. ¶ Returning to jewelry design skills she had first learned while attending Cranbrook, Kavanaugh created a series of earrings, brooches, and bracelets for ACME Studios in the 1990s. Founded in 1985, ACME was already famous for producing a collection of jewelry with the Memphis Group designers. Kavanaugh added her work to this esteemed collection alongside California designers that included April Greiman and Peter Shire. ¶ Finally, coming full circle back to her earlier holiday creations, in 2014 the national home goods retailer CB2 produced a geodesic, pyramidal Christmas tree Kavanaugh had originally designed in the 1960s—this time adorned with a newly designed line of anodized aluminum ornaments.

↓ This playful nativity scene was commissioned by Department 56 in the mid-2000s but was never produced.

↑ For the first incarnation of the Three Wise Men figures, Kavanaugh had a cabinetmaker cut shapes from solid wood, which she then painted. Almost fifty years later, she proposed a similar design to Department 56.

↑ Kavanaugh proposed these clip-on papier-mâché tree ornaments to Target in the late 2000s or early 2010s.

↑ Designed in the mid-1960s, this wooden cutout Christmas crèche was made as a gift for Kavanaugh's mother. The original was included in the 1968 exhibition *California Design Ten*. An updated version was created for Department 56 in the mid-2000s.

→ This wooden cutout Christmas crèche, from the 1950s or 1960s, was purchased for the collection of *Better Homes & Gardens* magazine.

A COLORFUL LIFE

→ This press photograph, taken to accompany coverage of Kavanaugh's Raku Gallery exhibition, highlights Kavanaugh's city planning toy — a set of wood blocks in the shapes of buildings, cars, and people, plus a square mat printed with a grid of roads. The prototype, made in the mid-1960s, resides in the collection of the Los Angeles County Museum of Art. A photograph of the complete set can be seen on page 168.

↑ Proposed in the mid-1960s for Department 56, this wooden schoolhouse was inspired by a Swedish mausoleum pictured in a photograph that Kavanaugh received from a friend.

→ This wooden Noah's ark from around 1965 was produced for an exhibition of Kavanaugh's work at Raku Gallery in Beverly Hills. It was also included in the Pasadena Art Museum exhibition *California Design Nine*. In this photograph Noah's wife has a flower in her hair "because she's going on a cruise." Noah had a hook in his hand "to catch any of his ark passengers who decided to jump ship."

This ACME Studio jewelry collection designed by Kavanaugh in the 1990s includes the Country Road earrings and brooch, Tee Pee earrings, and Santa Fe House brooch. ACME was the only company to work with all fourteen Memphis Group designers.

These slab ceramic floral plates are an example of an experiment Kavanaugh did in 2014 "for fun, in hopes that someone might catch on to them…usually about twenty years later." The plates rest on a linen fabric with leather dots, a previous example of her experimentation with materials.

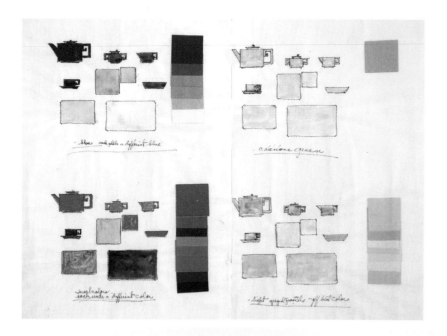

← This 1980s concept drawing depicts Kavanaugh's idea for a square dinnerware set for Carnevale, a Memphis, Tennessee, retailer. An ode to efficiency, the dishware was designed to fit compactly into standard kitchen cabinets. The project never went into production, so she later sold the concept to CB2.

↓ MOOD DINNERWARE, 2015. The name of this matte-glazed stoneware set comes from the 1930 jazz composition "Mood Indigo." The pieces were glazed in shades of blue, which according to Gere is the best color for food presentation.

" Gere possesses the rare skill of staying in touch with people. I would hear from Gere every several months with some interesting bit of news about something she had read in the *New York Times*, or some design show that was going on, or some interesting new restaurant or shop that was opening in Los Angeles. We would always have these wonderful conversations. Working in the corporate world can be somewhat enervating, and after I spoke to Gere, I would always feel so energized, inspired, and amazed by the enthusiasm she still had for discovery and ideas. Finally we had the chance to work together when I went to head up product development for the Christmas wholesaler Department 56. I was looking for some way to bring a fresh perspective to Christmas decor, and Gere came to mind. She LOVED the idea because she adores Christmas, and that was it. What resulted was this incredible collection of holiday decorations, including a set of Three Wise Men, a crèche, and a nativity wall-decor piece. ❋ Sadly, her Christmas designs never made it to market. But what did happen is a friendship that has grown over the years. ❋ A year or two later, I received in the mail a package from Gere that included a set of Wise Men and the nativity wall plaque. I couldn't believe it! They remain some of my very favorite things that I pull out every year when I start my holiday decorating. Due in part to their uniquely Gere Kavanaugh design aesthetic, but also due to how they came to be. " — Bridget Burke, Design Manager for Decorative Home, Target

"By 1964 I had become a design merchant because of my new store, Scarabaeus, on East Sixtieth Street in Manhattan, where the rich and famous came to visit and shop. My product sources and inventory were the driving spirit of the store. Product selections were unorthodox and came from unexpected resources, not in the normal stream of 'resource' for reselling. Through this process, I met several creative spirits and original thinkers whose ideas were ripe for commercial applications. ✽ My first exposure to the West Coast was through Norman Laliberté, whose works we were selling intensively. He connected us to the Immaculate Heart College in Los Angeles, where Sister Magdalen Mary and Sister Corita Kent were the inspirational gurus and leaders. ✽ Then followed my encounters with Gere Kavanaugh, Deborah Sussman, and Frank Gehry: three potential stars sharing one common space. Each of these personalities could have been developed (and exploited, to use a harsher word). Each one was groping into a career line, and each one had a different dimension, but they shared many ideas in common. As the multicultural third party in this trio, the one and only Gere Kavanaugh stood out through her remarkable style, demeanor, and personality. My longtime relationship with Gere was based not on business, but on shared thoughts, habits, and ideas. We held many subjects and styles in common interest. ✽ Gere has always been the ultimate chic lady with crisp and sophisticated gestures, language, aesthetics, and elegance. Later on in her career, she received recognition for her diversity of style and form, and she has tackled countless factions of design without ever having been pigeonholed. Gere is a vibrant free spirit, yet remains authoritative and decisive. She is truly an American icon of design." — George M. Beylerian, Founder, Material ConneXion

A look into the world of design

featuring Geré Kavanaugh

name it. She designs it.

...eewheeling artist Geré Kavanaugh ...a clock tower going up in Pitts-...h and a plant turning out aprons in ...hern California. This winter she'll ...Ireland to help the Irish Board of ...develop small craft industries. ...somewhere outside Seoul, Korea, ...tory is producing handwoven silks

with fabrics and looms both designed by Miss Kavanaugh.

"I took their tradition and related it to our times," she says. "You must live up to the moment, create for today.

"Antiques? What good designers are doing today will be the antiques of tomorrow. I don't buy them unless they are unique or humorous. Why rely on the

past? Let's live in today's terms."

Artist Kavanaugh would like to turn everybody's creativity on. "People must use their own ingenuity and imagination. Accepting everything like toothpaste out of a tube is all too prevalent today. We need as much emphasis on how to live well as on science and technology." CONTINUED

TEXT AND PHOTOGRAPHS
BY YVONNE MOZÉE

Article by Yvonne Mozée, *Pace* magazine, November 1968.

"I love to cook. My favorite culinary art is a Sunday morning 'brinner' of curried eggs in pastry shells with sparkling fruit punch served for lots of fr

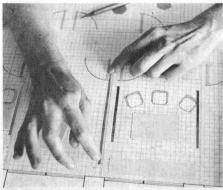

Floor plan of ad agency indicates furniture and facilities.

Showing what any homeowner can do, Miss Kavanaugh makes series of decorativ

38

"It is just as important to feed the soul visually as to feed the stomach."

Joseph Magnin's "Le Soupçon" is designed by Kavanaugh from place mats to umbrellas.

Geré Kavanaugh's studio and home are both in West Los Angeles, but her commitment to design began at the Memphis Academy of Arts at the age of eight. "It all started on Saturday afternoons. Father, who was a rare-book dealer, read and mother baked in the kitchen while the Metropolitan Opera played on the radio. I began to draw."

Lessons at the Academy developed into a scholarship. Then she took a master's degree in design at Cranbrook Institute in Detroit. Work with General Motors and then with the architectural firm of Victor Gruen preceded the setting up of her own studio five years ago.

"The designer's responsibility is wider today," she claims. "There are many more materials and people to deal with. Lighting, air conditioning, sound, television. A designer has to create the facilities so these things can function. There are even possibilities of pumping up a house as you inflate boats and chairs. In years to come we will be more nomadic, but I think we will still use the home as a focal point."

Future-oriented Miss Kavanaugh thinks ways of shopping are going to change. "There's a great longing for individuality and it's coming to a head in clothing. But some things don't need individuality, like blue jeans and underwear. These you can get by catalog or phone. Then when you do have time to go shopping, you want someplace special and unique." Working with two architects she has designed eight stores, each with a different look, for the Joseph Magnin chain in California.

But even though exhilarated about today Miss Kavanaugh has not abandoned the past. The stairway of her

Home serves up "visual food" to visitors.

home is hung with ancient and contemporary pieces—from Asia, Central America, North Africa, Italy. Inhabiting her high-ceilinged living room are Korean ceramics, miniature woodblocks for printing Indian fabrics, Mexican pottery and American Indian baskets. "Just having them around, looking at them out of the corner of my eye as I pass through the room, is food for me visually."

She feels the same about nature's products. Seashells freckle a window seat. Butterflies are mounted in a frame. A lacy dry bush hangs from the kitchen ceiling. The "strong and honest forms" in industrial areas, such as rolls of newsprint stacked up, also have an impact on her. Systems, ways of putting things together, are important too. "They trigger the mind," Geré says.

Cakes to clocks, toys to townhouses... for her, good design means good living

1 One-of-a-kind Noah's Ark handmade by Designer Geré Kavanaugh. "I'd like to design for tomorrow's trains and planes too," she says. "There's no pat solution in life—for school, marriage, family. It isn't that easy or that dull. Stay loose— keep open! You have to learn to walk on marbles."

2 Paper luncheon set. "If I could redo one thing in Los Angeles it would be Pico Boulevard. People wouldn't think of putting garbage in their stomachs but put garbage in their eyes all the time. There's a definite relationship between the exterior world and a person's inner life."

3 Prototype for table centerpieces with matching dessert plates. "Nonessential necessities make life really fun."

4 Geré's own Christ- mas card on Mylar. Kavanaugh-designed Christmas birthday cakes declaring "Happy Birthday Jesus" are sold by Blum's.

5 Model of 32-ft.-tall clock tower of silk- screened glass blocks for Monroeville Mall in Pitts- burgh, to be opened Feb. 1, 1969. "Being creative is starting out in one direc- tion, then going another, not knowing the totality or final outcome until you reach the end. You just follow your nose."

6 Settee of oak, wa and Haitian cotto "A good piece of furni is just as important as painting or book of po

7 "Rose in Korea" and other silks designed in Korea for Isabel Scott. "Theories on color are bunk. The no formula for anythin

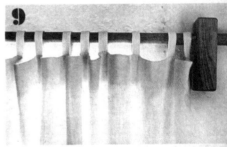

8 Hand-hooked rug took her two years to do. "My parents instilled in me a sense of quality. If you don't make it well, then don't bother."

9 Ash curtain rod. "Young people on budgets should get things they really love, one at a time if necessary."

10 Tile and wood dowel table designed for her living room and always topped with a bouquet of daisies. "If you can't work within a framework—budget, space limitations, etc.— you aren't a creative person. Creativity is doing the job to the best of your ability."

california
design

Between 1954 and 1976 the Pasadena Art Museum held
twelve *California Design* exhibitions, which showcased
"'implements of living' by designer craftsmen, industrial
designers, furniture designers, and California manufacturers." Funded by the County of Los Angeles to promote
California—and in particular Los Angeles—production
and manufacturing, these exhibitions both encouraged
natives to buy local and helped turn the nation on to
the state's distinctive offerings. ⁋ First organized by
Clifford Nelson, the *California Design* shows were turned
over to Eudorah Moore, design curator for the Pasadena
Art Museum, beginning with *California Design Eight* in
1962. Moore, who became a lifelong friend of Kavanaugh's,
upped the ante by forming juries comprising prominent
local designers and craftspeople to select the work.
She also began to produce striking exhibition catalogs. They featured photographs by Richard Gross of the
design objects in the California landscape, capturing a
certain local attitude of willful nonconformity. ⁋ The
California Design exhibitions were each organized into
two sections. One featured designs meant for mass production, and the other included objects made by individual
craftsmen (and craftswomen!). Kavanaugh's work was
included in *California Design Eight, Nine, Ten,* and *76*
(so named in celebration of the American bicentennial).
⁋ These legendary and highly anticipated exhibitions of
outrageous California craft announced that the Golden
State had arrived and was having its day in the national
sun. And Gere Kavanaugh was its golden girl.

↑↑ *CALIFORNIA DESIGN EIGHT* catalog, 1962.
↑ *CALIFORNIA DESIGN TEN* catalog, 1968.

↑↑ *CALIFORNIA DESIGN NINE* catalog, 1965.
↑ *CALIFORNIA DESIGN 76* catalog, 1976.

→ This city planning toy prototype was included in *California Design Ten* in 1968 and is now in the collection of the Los Angeles County Museum of Art.

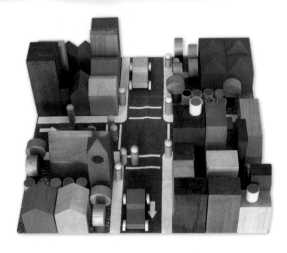

‹ These wooden clock tower blocks, made in the mid-1960s, were included in the *California Design Nine* exhibition and catalog.

→ These wallpaper designs from the 1960s were included in the *California Design Ten* exhibition and catalog. At top right, A Thousand Flowers, created for Bob Mitchell Designs, and at bottom right, Spice Flower, for Bill Keliehor Designs. Kavanaugh used this paper in her Joseph Magnin store design (see page 66).

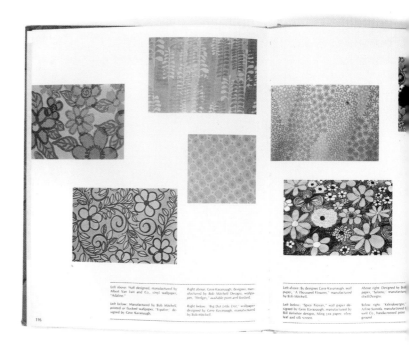

← HEDGES, 1960s. Produced for Bob Mitchell Designs, Hedges wallpaper was available printed or flocked.

← ESPALIER, 1960s. Also produced for Bob Mitchell designs, printed or flocked.

↓ BIG DOT LITTLE DOT, 1960s. Blue polka dots make up this sweet wallpaper produced for Bob Mitchell Designs.

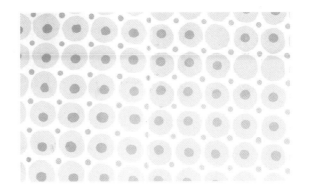

←↑ This floral rug hooked by Kavanaugh in 1965 was included in the "With an Accent on Color" section of *California Design Nine* and the exhibition catalog. Today Kavanaugh uses the rug in her home (see page 196).

←← This Richard Gross photograph of the Shaker Settee by Kavanaugh appeared in the opening spread of the "Accent on Seating" section of the *California Design Nine* catalog. The prototype for the settee was produced by craftsman David Edberg and now resides in Kavanaugh's home (see page 193).

...loz sings in a prototype rug hooked by Gere Kavanaugh; an upholstered fiberglass, aluminum ...e conference chair by George Kasparian; and a wood garden mural or divider by Joyce Aiken ...d Jean Ray Laury. The other side of the fence is painted in tones of blue and green.

...alifornia Design / 9 with an accent on Color / Pasadena Art Museum   1965   53

graphic design

The final arrow in Kavanaugh's quiver is graphic design, an area she first explored while creating her Cranbrook thesis project, for which she laid out and illustrated a number of children's books. She later cultivated her skills creating promotions for General Motors. These early experiences gave her the confidence to extend the range of her vision and services, allowing her to offer the entire "kit and caboodle." Navigating across disciplines for clients such as Isabel Scott Fabrics and Toys by Roy gave Kavanaugh the chance to explore different design techniques using a variety of materials. ⨍ For The Broadway, a Los Angeles chain of department stores, she was hired to focus exclusively on graphic design. Her experience in textiles shows in the bold patterns and shapes she employed throughout the company's design identity. ⨍ Materiality was often as important in her typographic work as it was in her textiles and spacial design. She imagined letters as topiaries (in her concept for Union Station signage); she created letters out of a curtain of gold discs (for the exhibition *Fantasy Clothes, Fantasy Costumes*); and it's no surprise that her type would end up as the icing on the cake—or in this case, the "Happy Birthday, Jesus" cake she created for Blum's. ⨍ For Kavanaugh, having a cross-disciplinary approach proved that what she can do has no boundaries; design is her vast playground.

→ In 1964, when she launched her own studio, Kavanaugh designed stationery that included a letterhead and envelope, a Rolodex card, and a shipping label. When she relocated to downtown Los Angeles in 1982, she designed her moving announcement. All were typeset by Vernon Simpson Typographers in Helvetica Thin.

gere'kavanaugh/designs
11632 san vicente boulevard
los angeles, california 90049

telephone 213 826-5215

gere'kavanaugh/designs
11632 san vicente boulevard
los angeles, california 90049

gere'kavanaugh/designs
11632 san vicente boulevard
los angeles, california 90049
telephone 213 826-5215

gere kavanaugh|designs
has moved to

420 boyd street
los angeles, california 90013
213 687 8270

architectural interiors, graphics, product development, exhibitions, architectural color, etc.

gere'kavanaugh/designs
11632 san vicente boulevard
los angeles, california 90049

Drawn and designed by
Kavanaugh, this 1985
set of Gere Kavanaugh/
Designs promotional
cards printed by Aardvark
Letterpress came
wrapped in a bellyband
with a metallic "Year of
the Dragon" label.

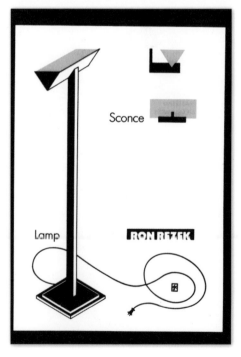

Recognized in the 1985 AIGA California juried competition, this packaging for The Broadway department store was designed in 1984. The project was art directed by Kavanaugh and designed and created by her staff: Cliff Lemon, Neal Taylor, and Lauren Kasmer. As part of the packaging concept, a variety of stickers in playful shapes and colors were designed to be applied to gift boxes.

gere's world

holiday craft

→ CHRISTMAS TREE, CA. 1972. Every year at the Memphis Academy of Arts Junior Saturday School, someone would craft a handmade tree. (One year it was made from ballerina tutus!) This festive tradition inspired Kavanaugh's prodigious lifelong output of Christmas ornaments and holiday decorations. This geometric tree was made with green garden sticks tied together with fuzzy pink pipe cleaners. Patterned bird and fruit ornaments were made from papier-mâché.

←← Shown are two of the seven or so colorways for the Tile Cross wrapping paper pattern Kavanaugh designed for CPS Industries in the mid–late 1970s, described in *House Beautiful* magazine as a "romantic derivation from the Iberian patterning of Portuguese tiles."

Christmas is Kavanaugh's special indulgence, and enthusiastically creating cards, ornaments, and crèches is her way of celebrating the season. "I grew up with Christmas being a very special holiday. Starting at Halloween, my father and I would shell the nuts for my mother to bake cookies...and we had cookies for breakfast until Valentine's Day." ¶ For many years Kavanaugh created handmade, labor-of-love holiday cards. These whimsical greetings were a way to reach out to her wide circle of friends and were collected as treasures. In 2015 CB2 turned one of Kavanaugh's holiday crafts, a modern design for a Christmas tree originally made from plastic drinking straws, into manufactured reality.

This wonderful assortment of handmade holiday ornaments from 1960 through the early 1970s includes fanciful papier-mâché birds with paper tail feathers, brilliantly colored papier-mâché disks and fruits, and abstract birds made from cut and screen-printed beer cans, folded and attached to wire hooks. The papier-mâché birds were created for an article in *Ladies' Home Journal.*

→ Kavanaugh silkscreened this holiday card with white ink on kraft paperboard in 1973. The red sun provides a pop of color.

↓ Letters set in Clarendon were silkscreened onto a purple greeting, which was then adorned with stickers for this holiday card from 1966.

Handmade Holiday Cards

Receiving festive mail from Kavanaugh is a joyous affair. This selection shows how she experimented with different media and printing techniques to create her fanciful handmade greeting cards.

↑ Kavanaugh designed this silkscreened card in 1968 after her first trip to Ireland, where she did some consulting for the Irish government. The text was inspired by a typical Irish greeting, which she encountered many times during her travels.

← The first in Kavanaugh's long tradition of Christmas cards, this three-color silkscreen print on gold paper was created around 1962.

to all the

cherubims

seraphims

blyth spirits of heaven and earth

the angels of Angelino Heights

wish you

a merry christmas

a happy holiday

and a glorious new year

god bless

Geraldine & Meeghan

↑ Designed after her move to Angelino Heights in 1980, this holiday greeting depicts Kavanaugh and her dog, Meeghan — complete with angel wings — standing in front of their new home. The card is adorned with metallic stickers, including a little Santa standing on the roof.

← This two-color screenprint on Mylar overlaid with pink tissue paper was made in 1967. Each card came with a circular, heart-laden tag.

↑ Made in 1966, this joyful
yellow card used a stamp
cut from a rubber inner
tube, with colorful confetti-
like squares of tissue paper
pasted on top.

→ A shimmering gold
card made in 1971 for all
Kavanaugh's Jewish friends.
Rabbi Leonard Berman
provided the translation with
a misspelling (it reads "Merry
Chritmas" in Hebrew), so all
the cards had to be reprinted.

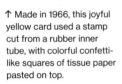

→ This silkscreen with
paper collage was sent
to special friends in 1969.
Zoos were a big source of
inspiration for Kavanaugh.
As a child she had lived
across the street from the
Memphis Zoo and walked
through it every day
on her way to school. She
spent a lot of time with
the animals, even feeding
them "onion grass" with
her father on weekends.
When the monkeys
smelled the Kavanaughs
coming they went crazy!

↑ A Kavanaugh-designed holiday
cake sold at Blum's, San Francisco
and Los Angeles, in 1967.

selby
avenue

→ A spring vision, Kavanaugh walks through her front door with a tote bag full of fresh flowers for a feature in the 1971 *LA Times* magazine article "Through the Doorway: A Strawberry Ice Cream Alcove."

→→ Hand-painted California oranges fill a telephone niche surrounded by luscious foliage. Both were applied with a powder puff sponge and outlined in black marker.

→ Fabric appliquéd with black felt, metal buttons, and large spangles covered Kavanaugh's bed and created a dramatic canopy.

Kavanaugh's homes have always been playgrounds, mixing her collections of folk art and crafts with furnishings and textiles of her own design. "What I like in a house is organized chaos," she said to *Women's Wear Daily* in 1969. "Everything I have has a special meaning. It all relates to my work." From around 1971 Kavanaugh lived on Selby Avenue in Los Angeles's Westside in a Spanish-style duplex designed by Parkinson & Parkinson (architects of the city's iconic Union Station and Bullocks Wilshire building). The princess of design ruled in her colorful palace. Adorning the archways between rooms were bold stripes inspired by both a double rainbow she had glimpsed on her travels in Ireland and the work of Frank Stella. Patterns of all shapes, scales, and hues collided in every room, creating a jubilant symphony. Purple and orange scalloped sculpture samples from her Fantasy Flowers project adorned the entrance. Her soft furnishings were upholstered in a variety of fabrics of her own design. Her handmade ornaments, including a geometric Christmas tree made from candy-striped drinking straws, hung from the ceiling. Evidence of Kavanaugh's work and collaborations was everywhere, proof that she lived with the things, images, and patterns that she created. She remained on Selby Avenue until around 1980, when she moved to the historic neighborhood of Angelino Heights near downtown Los Angeles.

in a house that glows throughout the *year*: 'good talk and good food are as necessary to me as the urge to create. In fact, they stimulate and sustain that urge'

For Titian-haired Southern California Designer Geré Kavanaugh—who makes no distinction between the joy of living and the pleasure of working—the art of entertaining is a bright and basic thread that appears throughout her busy professional life. "Good talk and good food are as necessary to me as the urge to create. In fact," she says, "they stimulate and sustain that urge."

As background for her richly variegated creative activities (she designs fabrics, ceramics, murals, sculptures, wallpapers, houses, offices, restaurants, exhibitions—and even town clocks), she chose this arched, white-walled Spanish townhouse for her home and studio. Part of a rambling enclave of five apartments, it gives her a just-right combination of privacy and communal security.

A house for all seasons, its spare interiors are an ideal foil for the colorful minglement of things—crafts, folk art, found objects—that she makes and collects. ("I'm a devout pack rat!") The simple architectural forms provide a neutral setting for an endless variety of informal entertaining arrangements.

An example of the flexible versatility of the house is seen in these two versions of the dining room. Set for a Christmas buffet breakfast (*left*), its chandelier and cloth-covered ceiling are festooned with silver tree ornaments. Arranged for a springtime sit-down supper (*right*), the chandelier becomes alive with a flight of white-paper doves and crepe-paper zinnias, all from Mexico.

GEORGE R. SZANIK

Although the house can receive large groups comfortably, Geré Kavanaugh prefers to limit her entertaining to no more than a dozen guests at a time. "A hostess can barely get around to talking to 10 or 12 people during the course of an evening and still do justice to serving them properly," she feels. But the visual impact (or "eye music," as Frank Lloyd Wright used to call it) of her parties gives them a gala sense of excitement that is usually associated with the bustle of much larger crowds.

The transformation of her living room from a serene, morning-filled space (*lower left*) to the flickering, candle-lit scene of a Christmas Eve party (*right*) is another instance of the range of the Kavanaugh lifestyle. The white sheepskin rug, the Marcel Breuer chairs and the round coffee table of her own design are still there but they have been invested with the glow of another world. Besides the addition of tapers and votive candles to every available surface, this metamorphosis was accomplished by the simplest of means. For example, the resplendent, starlike object that hangs just to the left of the arched entry is a wood ball drilled with holes and filled with Mexican candy suckers. It is suspended from the beam by a hank of yarn.

The arches, including those forming the connecting passage between living and dining rooms (*left*), are outlined with bold bands of color, not as an exercise in op art, but to commemorate a double rainbow she once saw in Ireland.

'a hostess can barely get around to talking to 10 or 12 people during the course of an evening and still do justice to serving them properly'

angelino
heights

Somewhere between a home and a museum, Kavanaugh's residence in Angelino Heights embodies the spirit of her life. From knocking down walls to designing her own furniture and crafting much of the decor, she has made it an evolving project for the past three decades (and she isn't finished with it yet). ¶ In the 1980s, when Kavanaugh purchased her home, the downtown Los Angeles neighborhood that had originally been a Victorian locale for the well-to-do was now considered a bit down-at-the-heels. Shortly after Kavanaugh moved in, she joined a community project to spruce the place up by planting myrtle trees, many of which still grow on her street. The orange trees in her backyard fill the air with the scent of citrus blossoms. Angelino Heights has changed over the years, but it's still a potpourri of distinctive characters, and Kavanaugh always bumps into someone she knows. Kavanaugh's sense of home extends far beyond her front door.

↑ A bright, activated living space full of collected treasures and an assortment of Kavanaugh's own designs, including this eclectic lighting fixture and many of her furniture prototypes. Featured in the foreground is her Zinnia table, made from irregularly shaped tiles that fit together—a daunting task for the tile producer. A variation of the table with marigold tiles and a different base can be seen farther back in the room.

← A floating blue Rudi Baumfeld credenza—a gift from the maker himself— is the stage for many ornaments and small sculptures made and collected over a lifetime. Above resides *Thumbelina*, a linoleum block print by Walter Anderson.

193

↓ According to Kavanaugh, these "curtains" made from drafting paper and painted like dotted swiss were meant as a joke.

↓↓ A window treatment made of chopsticks held together with paper and wire ties.

↑ A curated collection of baskets and tools selected as examples of intriguing craft and form hang in the kitchen entryway.

→ Skeleton leaves are delicately pinned on the front door window curtains.

↑ Kavanaugh's glass dining table perches on top of a white cube – an homage to Sol LeWitt – displaying a collection of gourds.

← A miscellany of teacups, all of which hold special meaning to Kavanaugh, are lined up on her shelves. The white-and-gold Frank Lloyd Wright reproduction mug is by Tiffany; some are from her childhood home; others are gifts or were collected during her travels. The square, stout, white teacup is Kavanaugh's own design, manufactured and sold by CB2.

← A small sample from Kavanaugh's enormous collection of teapots of many shapes and sizes fills the sideboard.

↓ A stack of hats sits atop an Arts and Crafts lamp that belonged to her mother.

← Three paintings done by Kavanaugh from the 1950s, including *Night Village* and *Bug*.

← Kavanaugh acquired this camphorwood chest when she was in South Korea designing for Isabel Scott Fabrics.

↑ This handhooked rug from 1965 took Kavanaugh more than a year to make. It was included in the *California Design Nine* exhibition and the recent exhibition *Golden State of Craft: California 1960–1985*.

← Kavanaugh hand crinkled these linen curtains by washing, wringing, and drying them in her backyard.

← Kavanaugh loves the Southwest and the iconography of the Spanish crucifix. She found some of these crosses while traveling in Santa Fe, a place she has often visited to see friends. Others came to her as gifts.

↑ This traditional Seminole Indian patchwork shirt, acquired in the 1980s or 1990s, reminds Kavanaugh of a skirt she owned as a girl.

↑ A trio of Salvadorian dolls made by "a grandmother out of scraps from a factory."

→ A photograph of Imogen Cunningham taken by Kavanaugh in the 1970s in Napa Valley.

→ A Jill Mitchell card featuring her hand-cut lettering.

→→→ A photograph taken at a Cranbrook reunion in the 2000s.

→→ A holiday greeting card from the creatives who shared studio space with Frank Gehry and his business partner, Greg Walsh, from 1965–74.

→ A note from the French Minister of Cultural Affairs, written in response to a letter Kavanaugh wrote about the ways that Paris had improved since her last visit.

→ A handwritten invitation from Wallace Berman to his 1960 gallery show.

→→ Kavanaugh was awarded the AIGA Medal in 2016 for a lifetime of outstanding work.

→ A note from Beverly Sills, renowned American opera singer.

→ A letter from journalist and political commentator Bill Moyers.

→ The back of a scribbled note from Frank Gehry.

←← A photograph from 1938 or 1939 pictures Victor Cusack (left) in his early twenties with Frank Lloyd Wright. It was a gift to Kavanaugh from Cusack.

← A silkscreened invitation to a party for Geraldine Fabrics, 1977.

←← A response from Buckminster Fuller, written after Kavanaugh had inquired about a toy she was designing, which was modeled after his geodesic dome.

← Jewelry designed for ACME Studios.

←← One of Kavanaugh's first art efforts, made in the second or third grade.

←←← An article on Kavanaugh's Angelino Heights home in the May 8, 2013, *New York Times*.

← A letter from Gerry Adams of Sinn Féin, Ireland.

← American Institute of Interior Designers, International Design Award for Kavanaugh's Koryo Clouds fabric designs, 1969.

HERO WALL. An ever-changing wall full of letters, clippings, photographs, and memorabilia celebrating special relationships and moments from Kavanaugh's full and colorful life.

❝ I met Gere Kavanaugh in 1986, when I had just moved back to Los Angeles after studying at the Basel School of Design in Switzerland. I'd heard that a studio downtown was looking for a designer, so I phoned Gere Kavanaugh/ Designs and, after a brief conversation, I had an interview. ✿ After just a few steps inside, I knew I had landed somewhere extraordinary. The studio was a visual and aural feast! There were product sketches, typographic sketches, floor plans, mobiles, cardboard prototypes, fabric samples, material samples, stone samples, toys, books, more books, more toys, and objects I didn't even recognize everywhere. Two dogs chased each other around the studio barking. I later found out that Bargain and Token were two in a long line of white, mop-like pooches that have always shared Gere's home and office. I thought, Yes! This is what design should be about. In Gere's world there are no disciplinary boundaries. Ever. ✿ I heard Gere before I ever saw her. That lilting, whooping laugh echoed through the office and suddenly, there she was: resplendent in beaded tennis shoes, a brightly quilted jacket of Asian origin, and flamboyantly ringed fingers. Gere leafed through my portfolio, exclaiming over letterforms I'd labored to paint by hand with a triple zero brush, and admiring a color palette that I'd chosen for a series of stamps with images of baroque churches. And, just like that, I had a job. That was thirty years ago. ✿ Gere has since become a treasured friend, but she's never stopped being my role model and mentor. She's forgotten more about design than I'll ever know and her joie de vivre is a lesson to us all. A hand-lettered poster she sent a few Christmases ago says it all: 'One lifetime is not enough!' ❞ — Terry Irwin, Head of the School of Design, Carnegie Mellon University

" As the young editor in chief for an erstwhile magazine called *Residential Interiors*, I planned a trip to LA. My mission was to find stories to tell about the free spirits that radiated to us, in the constricted East, from the adventurous West. Gere Kavanaugh came to my aid. She graciously invited the most interesting architects and interior designers in her city to meet me at her home, itself a design tour de force. The house was brimming with that great American optimism and generosity that caught my imagination as a young immigrant girl who found a new home in New Jersey. She lived (and still lives) with the kind of bright and inviting colors, patterns, and textures that were hard to find in a gray and neutral New York. And this was a great place for a party. By the end of the evening, I had met some of the most vibrant, active people at the center of LA's creative life, the kind of designers who continue to fascinate me to this day. As I left, my head was buzzing with the stories I'd write about them and their work. They filled up a whole issue of the magazine and graced future issues. " — Susan S. Szenasy, Director of Design Innovation, *Metropolis*

color studies & still lifes

Drawing has been an essential part of Kavanaugh's process throughout her career. For her, the joy of creating comes from the simple but wonderful act of putting pencil to paper. Kavanaugh made these pastel and colored-pencil drawings as a way to experiment with color palettes and composition without dealing with the pressing demands of a client. Though simple, these still lifes may also make references—to a box of yarn owned by Vincent van Gogh, for example, whose interest in color began after he encountered the threads of the Nuenen weavers. These images reflect and embody her gracious and colorful life.

·bennington· ·swirls· ·onion skins· ·cat's eyes· ·crackery china· ·agates· ·mitzes· ·common marbles·

" Gere's curiosity is insatiable. For the decade that I've been at LACMA Gere has been present at nearly every decorative arts and design event we've hosted. She is usually found in the front row and can be relied on to shoot her arm up in the air at the start of the Q&A period and ask the first, always provocative, question. " —Bobbye Tigerman, Curator of Decorative Arts and Design, Los Angeles County Museum of Art

" The booming voice saying 'helloooo' in the deli section of Gelson's market, the place where we mostly bumped into the 'grand lady' of all design. ✿ The extensive library and home filled with beautiful artifacts in every corner and with matching stories. (How did she ever find the time to read them all? But, in fact, I believe she did!) ✿ A person who would be at every and all design and art events, always with an opinion, too. ✿ A woman with an overwhelming passion for design, of all disciplines, and its history, and for a remarkably long time. ✿ An in-your-face critic with suggestions, requests, remarks, and demands. Someone you just have to love! **"** — April Greiman, Graphic Designer

index

Page numbers in pink refer to images.

←← PETIT FLEUR, 1976. Two of the many color palettes available in this pattern.

←← DAISY, CA. 1976. A variation on Gere's beloved signature motif.

Acknowledgments

This book began its embryonic stage in 2015 when Diana Murphy, then publisher and creative director at Metropolis Books, approached me about doing a series of books on the "California Girls" covered in my earlier volume, *Earthquakes, Mudslides, Fires & Riots: California and Graphic Design 1936–1986*. The series was not only to include Kavanaugh, but Deborah Sussman, Barbara Solomon Stauffacher, and Marget Larsen, among others. As I was itching for time to do further exploration of the careers and design work of these vibrant talents, it seemed ideal. For so many reasons, we decided the place to start was with Gere. We approached the grand dame of the Los Angeles design scene, and she generously opened her home and countless boxes and notebooks, files, and file drawers to our probing. That summer we were joined by Murphy's assistant, Jordan Steingard, and together we photographed, scanned, and recorded what seemed like Kavanaugh's endless and clearly prolific lifetime of production. We were awed at every turn.

But in 2016 Murphy departed from Metropolis and the owner felt the book might find a better home elsewhere. And it did. Thanks to Michael Carabetta, creative director for Chronicle Books, when he introduced the project to his Princeton Architectural Press colleague Sara McKay. She was a joy to work with as she shepherded the project along until it landed in very capable hands of editor Sara Stemen.

Neal Taylor, Gere's assistant, has been our godsend, negotiating every twist and turn and need—he practically willed this project into being.

But aside from Kavanaugh and Taylor, the sun that has shined brightest on the project for the longest time has been Kat Catmur, the book's coauthor and codesigner. There couldn't have been a more ideal partner: patient, persistent, good-natured, and extraordinarily talented as both a writer and designer, and SO much more. This book's exceptional glow is thanks to her.

The contributions of photographers Jennifer Cheung and Steve Nilsson cannot be overstated. They took on the challenges of documenting Kavanaugh's work, and without them there would simply be no book.

Along the way there have been many other generous contributors. My California Institute of the Arts student Audrey Davies joined us early on to walk Gere through the morass of images and questions and record Gere's thoughts; Andrew Blauvelt, Leslie Edwards, Gina Tecos, and Judy Dyki at Cranbrook have been exceptionally helpful and supportive; and then there's the collaborator that got away, Jessica Fleischmann. I'm extremely grateful for the help and support from Susan Skarsgard, Ellen Magnin Newman, Emma Kemp, Bill Stern, California Institute of the Arts, the office of Frank Gehry, Gruen Associates, Corey Reynolds, Alisa Benfey, Nancy Louise Jones, Anne Thompson, Tom Kracauer, Janet Sager Knott, Cheryle Robertson, Christine Steiner. And finally, everything good is made possible by my husband, Michael Shapiro.

Throughout the three years it took to realize the project, Kavanaugh has been at the ready with tea, cookies, and a steady laugh as we invaded her space time and again. As a designer myself, and knowing Gere as well as I've been privileged to know her, the patience this project demanded has been substantial. This natural raconteur had to trust us to tell her story and to design its container. It was heroic on her part. Hopefully we've done her justice.

Credits

All work by Gere Kavanaugh: © Gere Kavanaugh. 1, 64 top right: © the Estate of Ruth Asawa, courtesy the Estate of Ruth Asawa and David Zwirner; digital scans BowHaus. 2–8, 22, 23, 44–45, 48, 70 center left, 70 center right, 70 bottom left, 80 bottom, 81 bottom, 83 bottom left, 83 bottom center, 83 bottom right, 85 center right and left, 85 bottom, 88 top left, 92 top right, 93 top, 93 bottom left, 96 bottom, 102, 104 bottom left, 105–7, 114, 115, 117–19, 123–25, 128 bottom, 129, 130 bottom left, 130 bottom right, 131, 133 right, 135–41, 145 top right, 145 bottom, 147–49, 154 left, 155, 156, 173, 175, 179, 182 bottom right, 185, 218, 220–22: courtesy Gere Kavanaugh. 12, 20, 21, 24, 25, 58, 59, 78 bottom, 79, 80 top, 80 center, 81 top, 82, 83 top, 83 center, 85 top, 86, 87 (background), 88 top right, 88 center, 88 bottom, 89, 92 top left, 92 bottom left, 92 bottom right, 93 center left, 93 center right, 93 bottom right, 94, 95, 96 top, 97, 116, 126–27, 153, 157, 158, 167–71, 174, 176, 177, 180–81, 182 top, 182 bottom left, 183, 184, 193–99, 210, 211: courtesy Gere Kavanaugh; photos © Jennifer Cheung. 14: photo by Bruce M. White; © Lloyd E. Cotsen, 2016. 26, 27: courtesy Gere Kavanaugh; © Cranbrook Archives; photos by Harvey Croze. 28 top left, 28 center right, 28 bottom right, 29–31: courtesy Gere Kavanaugh/Cranbrook Academy of Art. 28 top right, 28 center left, 28 bottom left, 32–35: courtesy Gere Kavanaugh/ Cranbrook Academy of Art; photos © Jennifer Cheung. 36–40, 42–43: courtesy General Motors. 41: courtesy Gere Kavanaugh and General Motors. 47: *Christian Science Monitor*; courtesy Gere Kavanaugh. 49–55, 62–63, 64 top left, 64 center, 64 bottom, 65–69, 103: courtesy Gere Kavanaugh and Gruen Associates. 60: photo © Marvin Rand Estate, digital image © Jennifer Cheung. 61: Penske Media Corporation; photos by Nick Ackerman; courtesy Gere Kavanaugh; digital image © Jennifer Cheung. 70 top, 70 bottom right, 71: courtesy Gehry Partners, LLP. 72–73: Penske Media Corporation; photos © Marvin Rand Estate; courtesy Gere Kavanaugh; digital images © Jennifer Cheung. 77, 84, 154 right:

photos © Fritz Taggart Estate. 78 top: photo by Les Cooper. 87 (clipping): *Buffalo Evening News*; courtesy Gere Kavanaugh. 90–91: courtesy Gere Kavanaugh; photos © Jay Ahrend Photographs; digital images © Jennifer Cheung. 98–99: Hearst Communications, Inc.; courtesy Gere Kavanaugh; digital images © Jennifer Cheung. 128 top, 130 top, 132–33, 142–44, 224: photographs © Jennifer Cheung. 101: photos by Balthazar Korab. 104 top, 104 bottom right: courtesy Stanford Libraries Special Collections, © the Estate of Ruth Asawa, courtesy the Estate of Ruth Asawa and David Zwirner. 108–9: photos by Julius Shulman, courtesy Getty Research Institute, 2004.R.10. © J. Paul Getty Trust. 110–11: Hearst Communications, Inc.; photos by Max Eckert; courtesy Gere Kavanaugh; digital images © Jennifer Cheung. 112–13: Hearst Communications, Inc.; courtesy Gere Kavanaugh; photos © Elyse Lewin; digital images © Jennifer Cheung. 120, 121: photos © Lisa Romerein. 145 top left, 203–7: courtesy Gere Kavanaugh; jimsimmonsphotography.com. 146: © CAFAM; courtesy Gere Kavanaugh; digital image © Jennifer Cheung. 150–51: Sandow Publication. 161–65: photos by Yvonne Mozée; digital images © Jennifer Cheung. 187: photos © Elyse Lewin. 188–91: *House Beautiful*; courtesy Gere Kavanaugh; digital images © Jennifer Cheung. 219: courtesy Gere Kavanaugh; photo © Craig Cowan Estate. 223: Perfect Image; courtesy Museum of California Design.

Bios

Louise Sandhaus teaches in the Graphic Design program at California Institute of the Arts and is the author of *Earthquakes, Mudslides, Fires & Riots: California and Graphic Design, 1936-1986*.

Kat Catmur is a graphic designer from the UK who works predominantly in the cultural sphere. Her clients include the City of Los Angeles Department of Cultural Affairs, California Institute of the Arts, and the BBC.

PUBLISHED BY
Princeton Architectural Press
A McEvoy Group company
202 Warren Street
Hudson, New York 12534
www.papress.com

Princeton Architectural Press is a leading publisher in architecture, design, photography, landscape, and visual culture. We create fine books and stationery of unsurpassed quality and production values. With more than one thousand titles published, we find design everywhere and in the most unlikely places.

EDITOR: Sara Stemen
DESIGNERS: Kat Catmur and Louise Sandhaus
PREPRESS: Valerie Kamen and Ana Kaliski
PERMISSIONS: Cheryle Robertson, CTRclearances

TYPEFACES
Pitch, Klim Type Foundry. Designer: Kris Sowersby
Neue Haas Grotesk, Linotype. Designer: Max Miedinger and Christian Schwartz

SPECIAL THANKS TO: Paula Baver, Janet Behning, Abby Bussel, Benjamin English, Jan Cigliano Hartman, Susan Hershberg, Kristen Hewitt, Lia Hunt, Jennifer Lippert, Sara McKay, Parker Menzimer, Eliana Miller, Wes Seeley, Rob Shaeffer, Marisa Tesoro, Paul Wagner, and Joseph Weston of Princeton Architectural Press — Kevin C. Lippert, publisher

Library of Congress Cataloging-in-Publication Data
NAMES: Sandhaus, Louise, 1955– author. | Catmur, Kat, author. | Cheung, Jennifer, photographer (expression)
TITLE: A colorful life: Gere Kavanaugh, designer / Louise Sandhaus and Kat Catmur ; original photography by Jennifer Cheung.
DESCRIPTION: First edition. | New York : Princeton Architectural Press, 2019. | Includes index.
IDENTIFIERS: LCCN 2018026560 | ISBN 9781616897628 (hardcover : alk. paper)
SUBJECTS: LCSH: Kavanaugh, Gere, 1929– | Designers – United States – Biography. | Women designers – United States – Biography.
CLASSIFICATION: LCC NK839.K38 S26 2019 | DDC 741.6092 [B] – dc23
LC record available at https://lccn.loc.gov/2018026560

CAPTIONS FOR
FOLLOWING PAGES

P218 Top: This photograph was taken at an early 1970s birthday party for Deborah Sussman, just after she had received two bouquets of flowers from Ray Eames. Sussman is second from right, in a white hat. Kavanaugh is fourth from the left, in sunglasses.

P218 Bottom: A holiday greeting card from the creatives who shared studio space on San Vicente Boulevard, Los Angeles 1965–74. From left to right are Greg Walsh, Deborah Sussman, Steve Schuck, Gordon Sommers, Ron Rezek, Alan Torsman, Gere Kavanaugh, Babs Altoon, Xabi Aboritz, Lea Torchymann, and Frank Gehry.

P219: Photographer Craig Cowan shot Kavanaugh and her dog, Ms. Token, in the 1990s. Kavanaugh remembers with amusement that he asked to take her portrait because he found her "glamorous." When she showed up with a dirty sweater, he was even more impressed by her audacity.

P220: Gere Kavanaugh cheerfully peeks through a hole in one of her Fantasy Flowers around 1970.

P221 Top: Kavanaugh and her staff pictured at the Gere Kavanaugh/ Designs studio in Little Tokyo, Los Angeles, 1980s. Standing next to Kavanaugh is architect Cliff Lemon, while behind her stand Lauren Kasmer and Neal Taylor. Seated at desk is Linda Jacobson.

P221 Bottom: Kavanaugh and architect Paul Prejza surrounded by design studies for the 1984 Olympic Games.

P222: Kavanaugh's holiday greeting from 2009–10 encapsulates her often-expressed sentiment.

P223: A surprise hug from former colleague and studio mate Frank Gehry on October 25, 2015, at the Museum of California Design's Henry Awards honoring the legendary architect's body of work.

P224: An always-welcoming Kavanaugh in the entryway of her Angelino Heights home, wearing a dress and fabric of her own design, 2017. Not pictured, her rubber-chicken purse, just out of view.

Greg Walsh · Steve Schenck · Gordon Sommers · Alan Swanson · Babs Altoon · Louis Olivier · Harold D. Gooley

Ron Regal · Deborah Sussman · Gret Kavanaugh · Lea Torchmann

greetings!

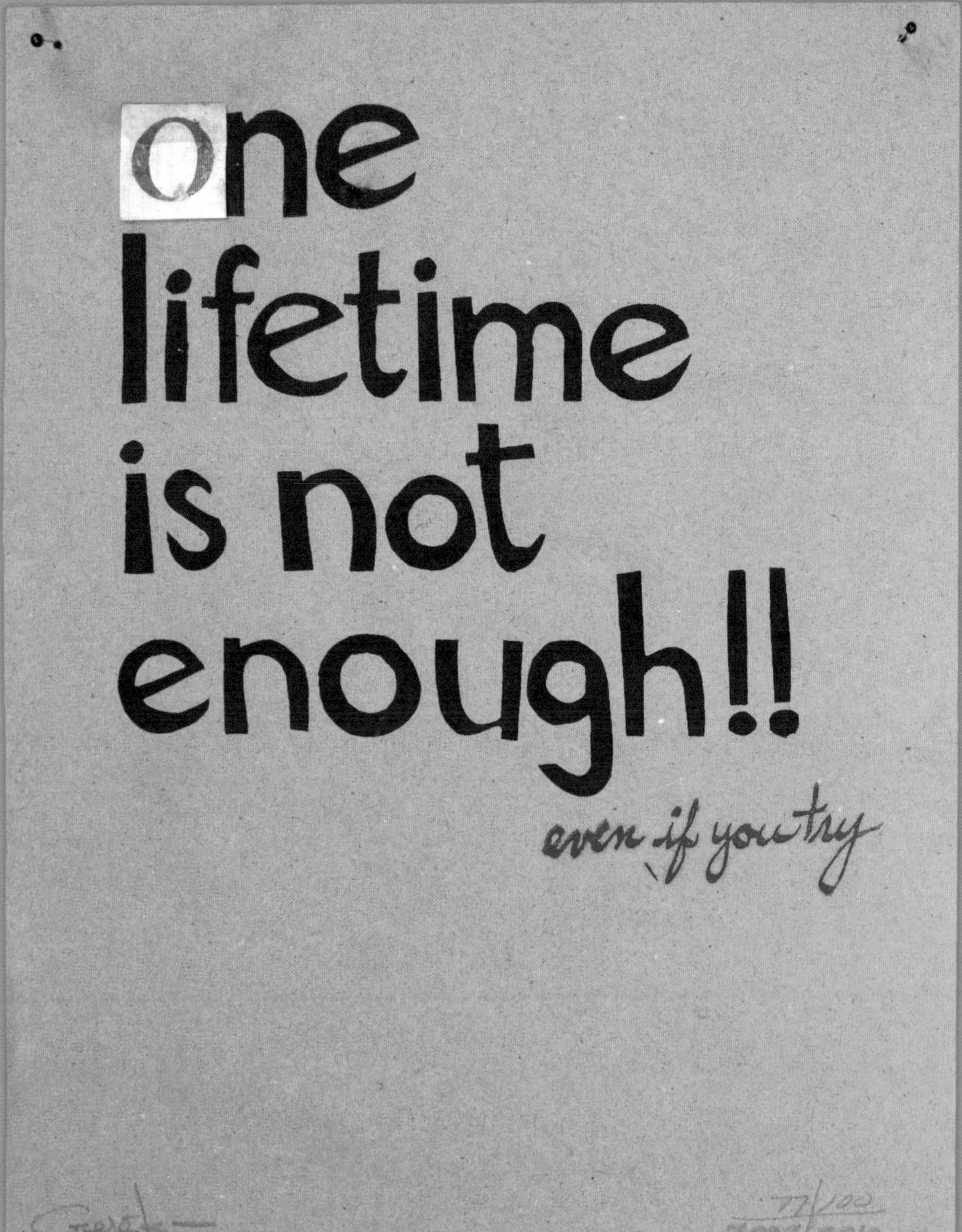
One
lifetime
is not
enough!!
even if you try
77/100
2009/2010